A TASTE OF
MONTANA

Favorite Recipes from Big Sky Country

by **Seabring Davis**

photography by Paulette Phlipot
foreword by Greg Patent

FARCOUNTRY
PRESS

❧ For my mother, who taught me how to cook. ❧

ISBN 10: 1-56037-562-0
ISBN 13: 978-1-56037-562-3

© 2013 by Farcountry Press
Text © 2013 by Seabring Davis
Photography © 2013 by Paulette Phlipot
Photography © 2013 by Jason Savage on back cover and pages ii and iii

For more information on our books, write Farcountry Press, P.O. Box 5630,
Helena, MT 59604; call (800) 821-3874; or visit www.farcountrypress.com.

Library of Congress Cataloging-in-Publication Data

Davis, Seabring,
  A taste of Montana : favorite recipes from Big Sky Country / written by
Seabring Davis ; photography by Paulette Phlipot.
      pages cm
  Includes index.
  ISBN 978-1-56037-562-3 -- ISBN 1-56037-562-0
1. Cooking, American. 2. Cooking, American--Western style. 3.
Cooking--Montana. I. Title.
  TX715.D265125 2013
  641.59786—dc23
                                    2013021218

Created, produced, and designed in the United States. Printed in China.

17 16 15 14 13   1 2 3 4 5

contents

chapter 1: Breakfast & Brunch

chapter 2: Appetizers & Snacks

chapter 3: Salads & Sides

chapter 4: Soups & Stews

chapter 5: Main Courses

chapter 6: Desserts & Sweet Treats

chapter 7: Cook's Pantry

acknowledgments

by Seabring Davis

As with any good recipe, the quality of ingredients is what makes or breaks a dish. If this cookbook is "the dish," then I feel it was possible only because I started with the very best ingredients. Also essential were the gracious chefs, restaurants, bars, hotels, ranches, and inns that took the time to contribute their recipes to the book. Thank you, especially to the J Bar L Ranch, Buck's T-4 Lodge, Chico Hot Springs, Lone Mountain Ranch, the Garden Wall Inn, 2nd Street Bistro and Gil's Goods, and the Sacajawea Hotel. If not for the love of food, people, and diversity in the kitchen, we wouldn't have such great places throughout the state to share a meal.

To all the hardworking farmers and ranchers—big and small—in Montana, thank you. Every bit of agricultural land in the state preserves open spaces that are essential to our quality of life. Thank you also to the Western Sustainability Exchange in Livingston for growing a unique and friendly farmers' market.

I'm grateful to photographer Paulette Phlipot for her sumptuous images, which carry this book to a higher level. She is ever the professional, both talented and tireless!

Thank you to Kathy Springmeyer, Jessica Solberg, Will Harmon, Shirley Machonis, and the rest of the team at Farcountry Press. Their patience and assistance along the way were invaluable. I appreciate all the hard work the publishing staff put toward creating such a beautiful book.

Finally, my family deserves the most credit for helping with this book. My husband, Colin, is not only a fantastic "dish dog" when the sink is piled with "testing" dishes, but he is a true foodie and my best friend. My daughters, Isabel and Simone, approve of all these recipes; they are excellent tasters. And thank you to my friends, for being great eaters, encouragers, and companions through the deadline crunches. Always. *Bon appétit!*

by Paulette Phlipot

I would like to thank the team at Farcountry Press, especially Shirley Machonis, Jessica Solberg, Kathy Springmeyer, and Will Harmon. It's been such an honor to be a part of another Farcountry cookbook. The adventures, tastes, and friendships that I gained from photographing this book have given me a greater appreciation and understanding of really how unique and magical the state of Montana is. Such a beautiful place, with very friendly people, and food full of history and love.

I am very grateful for meeting and having the opportunity to work with Seabring Davis. I've never seen someone cook as much food in one day or multitask like she can, and all the while everything she touches turns beautiful. Seabring's talent and style added so much to so many of the photographs in the book. I am forever thankful for the kindness and hospitality she and her beautiful family embraced me with throughout my travels to Montana.

The best part of working on a book like this is being able to visit the places and meet the people behind the food. Oh how I wish I could have visited each and every one who contributed to this book! For those I did visit, I want to thank you for welcoming me and my camera with open arms. And a special thanks to Pamela Sinclair, author of *A Taste of Wyoming*—thank you for creating the first book in this series of wonderful cookbooks!

foreword

by Greg Patent

Montana is the fourth largest state, and agriculture is its number one industry. Some of the best beef in the country is raised here, and the state's rich farmland yields abundant crops of wheat, lentils, barley, and oats. With numerous farmers' markets, summertime offers fresh produce to both restaurant chefs and home cooks and gives folks a chance to get to know the people who grow their food.

In this celebratory cookbook, Seabring Davis shares her experiences as she traveled the state to interview chefs and sample their creations. What were they cooking? Why did they choose these dishes? She learned that these chefs cook seasonally as much as possible and use the freshest ingredients. They opt for vegetables, fruits, and dairy products from local farms; they forage for wild mushrooms and huckleberries; their menus feature pheasant, deer, and elk; they purchase beef, lamb, bison, and chicken from in-state ranches; and they buy artisanal cheeses and sausages from local producers.

Fifty-eight recipe contributors and forty-five regional producers are represented in this book. All of them are committed to fostering the important farm-to-table movement that brings healthy, sustainably raised foods to the dinner table in the shortest distance possible. Given the vastness of Montana, this is no mean feat. Yet as the saying goes, Montana still feels like a small town with a long Main Street.

The 110 recipes here are clearly and invitingly written, and completely do-able by the home cook. Seabring's generosity of spirit shines through with the helpful tips she gives on utensils, equipment, and how to test for doneness. Her advice on high-altitude baking is especially helpful.

A Taste of Montana is so much more than a book of recipes. It reveals a bountiful state whose food supply is a wonderful work in progress, and it showcases innovative chefs who find new flavors in local foods. Seabring inspires the home cook to remember that cooking and eating are pleasures to be savored and appreciated.

Greg Patent is the author of several beloved cookbooks, including Baking in America, *which won the 2003 James Beard Award. He cooks and writes from his home in Missoula, Montana.*

introduction

*"You don't have to cook fancy or complicated masterpieces—
just good food from fresh ingredients."*

—JULIA CHILD

Food is a journey. It's a daily excursion I take by thinking about the value of what we eat. Where does it grow? How will I cook it? What will taste good with it? From the moment food comes to my kitchen, I love the process of planning a home-cooked meal, preparing each element, then serving and savoring the results with people I love.

I'd love to tell you that I am a chef with impressive professional credentials, and that I could dazzle you with my cooking technique and wow you with my culinary expertise, but that's not me. The truth is, I am a journalist who loves to eat and cook. I write about food. I cook it. I eat it.

Don't misunderstand—I do have experience. I have taken and taught cooking courses. I have worked in commercial kitchens (once, during a bout of vegetarianism, I worked at a steak house preparing enormous prime rib beef roasts for the Sunday specials!) and know the nature of restaurant life. I have traversed thousands of miles of this state in search of great pie. I often drive 100 miles just for dinner, and I brake for farmers' markets.

It's true, I am likely to enter a recipe into the Yellowstone Food Festival or to daydream of winning a blue ribbon for my pie at the annual Park County Fair (alas, my pie crusts are never good enough!), but really, my food journey takes me to the grocery store. Even in that most domestic routine, it's a pleasure to consider interesting, healthy foods to feed my family. I take note that our sandwich bread is made from wheat grown in Montana. I look at fresh foods and consider how far they've traveled to my table. I try to support the farmers and ranchers in my community, my state—at the very least in the United States.

In the fleeting Montana summer I cook from the garden. Our small backyard plot is a gift—to harvest a salad minutes before eating it, to enjoy the aroma of fresh herbs and tomatoes, to savor the sweet crunch of carrots, peas, and peppers. Even the dream that, some day, one of those watermelon plants might bear even the tiniest fruit in the most impossible of growing conditions is a thrilling prospect. But most of our fresh

seasonal food comes from the local farmers' market along the Yellowstone River in Livingston. After the market one day, shucking corn for dinner with my daughters, I said, "This corn was picked just this morning." My kids looked at me, incredulous, "How do you know that?" I smiled with satisfaction and said, "I talked to the farmer."

It's important to talk to the farmer. It's important to know that our food is grown nearby. Supporting local producers is essential for the economic health and environmental benefits that we all reap.

Montana still boasts agriculture as its number one industry. For this reason, I've showcased recipes with specific Montana ingredients. Look through the book to find them and also the "Meet the producer" sidebars, which feature a handful of the hardworking businesses dedicated to growing and raising the food we eat.

The focus on the farm-to-table movement punctuates the importance of using fresh ingredients, while profiling the producers adds a "cultural" depth that reflects the unique character of this state. In fact, Montana arguably still holds claim to its "Big Sky Country" moniker in part because more than 90 percent of the private land in the state is either farms or ranches. Cattle and sheep ranches, rolling grain fields, bison ranches, cherry orchards, organic gardens and farms, dairies, pig and goat productions, and eggs from free-range chickens are at the heart of Montana's agricultural diversity. Visiting a farm, seasonal market, or food shop to support Montana's harvest is about more than just food; it's a means of preserving Montana's culture, open space, and economy. Plus, the result is delicious.

The culture of food in Montana is evolving. Even at a time when large farms and ranches are on the decline nationally, small farms in the West are increasing steadily. It is, in fact—without too much extra effort—possible to prepare a dinner with ingredients produced entirely in the state. The menu might look like this:

Appetizer:	Trout Meunière
Salad:	Roasted Beet Salad with Black Pepper Vinaigrette
Main Course:	Braised Montana Lamb Shanks with Black Beluga Lentils
Dessert:	Rustic Flathead Cherry Tart made with Wheat Montana pastry flour and local butter, topped with whipped cream from Kalispell Kreamery or Darigold.

That's a selection of food that would stand up in any restaurant, anywhere, and you can make it at home, and without letting your dollars leave the state.

Home is where most of my cooking is done. I cook almost every night of the week. I love a good dinner party. Rarely do I rely on step-by-step recipes; to me they are mere suggestions and inspirations. That is why this book is such a treasure to me—I have tested every recipe. Now I can revel in the fact that I have made chicken pâté, pheasant Marsala, potato gnocchi, and a coconut cream pie that my neighbors are still talking about. It has been a master course in cooking and a wonderful tour of restaurants in Montana that I hope will inspire your own efforts.

The recipes range from simple to complex and everything in between. Notice the diversity of recipes, from Wild West Pizzeria's Mac and Cheese dinner, to the involved preparation of Barbecue Bison Short Rib Ravioli from the chef at Chico Hot Springs Resort. Focusing on the farm-to-table movement, I've highlighted many restaurants that incorporate fresh, local ingredients and profiled a few Montana producers who deserve recognition. There are many other Montana sources listed in the Sources chapter at the back of the book. I hope you'll seek out the restaurants, farms, and ranches mentioned here as you continue your own food journey—there's nothing complicated or fancy, just good food from fresh ingredients.

—Seabring Davis

guidelines for recipes

Equipment:

- ❧ Oven temperatures are given in degrees Fahrenheit. For best results, always preheat your oven when instructed to do so.

- ❧ Most recipes were developed and tested using professional ranges, so adjustments in cooking and baking times may be necessary for home preparation. To test baked goods for doneness, insert a toothpick into the center of the baked product and remove it. If it comes out clean, the product is ready to come out of the oven.

- ❧ A stand mixer (a motorized appliance with a bowl and inter-changeable mixing tools, typically a dough hook, paddle, and whisk) is a nice luxury in the kitchen, but a hand mixer will work just as well for most recipes.

High-Altitude Cooking and Baking:

At sea level, air density is higher, and as elevation increases, air density decreases. All of these recipes were developed at high-altitude locations, which affects cooking and baking in two ways:

- ❧ Water and other liquids boil at lower temperatures and evaporate quicker. Cooking time is longer.

- ❧ Leavening gases in breads and cakes expand more.

Since these recipes were developed and tested at elevations of 3,000 feet, adjustments may be required when preparing these recipes *below* 3,000 feet. Most won't need any adjustments, and I recommend following the recipe as written first. If needed, however, here are some changes that could improve the end results:

- ❧ Increase baking powder and baking soda: for each teaspoon listed, increase an additional ⅛ teaspoon.

- Increase sugar: for each cup of sugar listed, add 1 to 2 tablespoons.

- Decrease liquid: for each cup of liquid listed, reduce 1 to 2 tablespoons (excluding oils).

- Lower oven temperature 20 to 25 degrees. Note that baking time also may need to be adjusted, so watch products closely rather than following recipe directions for cooking and baking times.

Ingredients:

- The fresher the better.

- Butter refers to unsalted whole butter, unless otherwise noted. For best results, do not substitute unless the recipe indicates otherwise.

- Standard egg size is Large, Grade A. For best results use local farm eggs.

- Flour refers to unbleached white flour, preferably grown and milled in Montana.

- Milk refers to whole cow's milk. For best results, do not substitute unless the recipe indicates otherwise.

- Sugar refers to granulated sugar, unless otherwise noted.

- One tablespoon of fresh herbs is equal to 1 teaspoon dried.

- Use a medium-size lemon for recipes calling for lemon juice and zest. A medium-size lemon yields about 2 tablespoons of juice and 1 tablespoon of zest.

- See a list of Montana sources for specialty ingredients on page 142.

Preparation:

- ❧ "Standard" recipes for sauces, doughs, and other basic items associated with specific recipes in the book are found in the Cook's Pantry chapter beginning on page 125.

- ❧ Diced indicates cutting into ¼- to ½-inch cubes.

- ❧ Confit, which literally means "confetti" in French, generally means food prepared into small pieces—hand torn or diced.

- ❧ Sauté means to cook ingredients cut into small pieces (such as diced, versus a large piece of meat, which would be pan fried) with a small amount of fat.

Utensils:

- ❧ Use a standard meat thermometer to test for desired doneness. Most meats are prepared medium-rare in these recipes.

- ❧ The Bundt pan size for these recipes is 9 x 3 inches (holds 8 to 9 cups); substitute an 8 x 8-inch square pan if needed.

- ❧ A sheet pan is a heavy-duty baking sheet; for home use it measures 13 x 9 inches and 1 inch deep.

- ❧ A small mixing bowl holds about 3 cups, a medium mixing bowl 6 cups (1½ quarts), and a large mixing bowl 10 cups (2½ quarts) or more. As Julia Child said, "Always start with a bowl that is bigger than you think you'll need."

- ❧ A sauté pan has flared sides, while a skillet has straight sides.

- ❧ A saucepan is deep enough to hold liquids. A small pan holds 4 cups (1 quart), a medium pot 8 to 10 cups (2 to 2½ quarts), and a large pot 20 cups (5 quarts).

Breakfast & Brunch

Parmesan Pain Perdu Benedict, p. 9

1 large bunch Lacinato (Dino) kale

4 cups diced potatoes

4 tablespoons extra virgin
    olive oil, divided

1 onion, sliced

Sea salt

16 fresh eggs, whisked

Dash half-and-half

3 cups grated Cheddar cheese

1 tablespoon minced fresh parsley

8 (12-inch) flour tortillas

Serves 8

❧ *Chef's Tip: Chiffonade is a technique for finely slicing leafy herbs into elegant ribbons. To do it, de-stem the leaves, roll, and then slice thin across the roll.*

❧ *Chef's Tip: These burritos freeze well. Wrap each burrito loosely in foil and freeze in a tightly closed container. To reheat, bake in a 325-degree oven for 25 minutes.*

Breakfast Burrito with Caramelized Onion, Roasted Potato, and Crispy Kale

NORRIS HOT SPRINGS, NORRIS
CHEF/PROPRIETOR HOLLY HEINZMANN

Not many experiences beat a morning soak at this local hot springs. The sun just barely peeks above nearby Bear Trap Canyon, the steam roils off the surface of the outdoor pool, the veggies are fresh from the greenhouse, the birds are chirping to start the day, and breakfast is served poolside. Life is good.

Preheat the oven to 400 degrees. Wash and spin the kale. Spread the leaves in a single layer on paper towels to dry completely. Toss the potatoes in 2 tablespoons of olive oil and roast them on a baking sheet in a single layer until tender, about 20 minutes. Shake the pan every 10 minutes for even cooking.

Over medium heat, caramelize the onions in 1 tablespoon of olive oil, scraping the pan as the onions brown, 15 to 25 minutes.

Chiffonade the kale into bite-size pieces and toss with the remaining 1 tablespoon of olive oil. Spread the kale pieces in a single layer on a baking sheet and sprinkle lightly with sea salt. Roast until crispy, not browned, 10 to 15 minutes, shaking the pan every 5 minutes.

Mix the eggs with the half-and-half and scramble in a separate skillet until almost done; remove from heat.

Combine the scrambled eggs, crispy kale, caramelized onions, roasted potatoes, grated cheese, and fresh parsley in a large bowl. Spoon into the center of each tortilla, dividing the mixture evenly. Tuck the bottom of each tortilla over the filling and roll it up, taking care to tuck in the sides as you roll.

Place the burritos on a baking sheet on the oven's center rack. Bake until heated through and the tops are lightly toasted, 3 to 5 minutes.

Rolls

1 ½ cups milk

½ cup (1 stick) butter, halved

1 teaspoon salt

2 eggs

¼ cup honey

¼ cup warm water

1 tablespoon yeast

3 to 4½ cups flour

1 cup sugar

3 tablespoons cinnamon

Icing

1 cup powdered sugar

1 teaspoon vanilla extract

¼ to ½ cup milk

Makes 1 dozen

Cinnamon Rolls

CRAZY MOUNTAIN INN, MARTINSDALE
CHEF CHERYL MARCHI

The wood-burning stove is always lit at the Crazy Mountain Inn. This end-of-the-road hotel and restaurant are worth an excursion off the beaten path. Appreciated among those in the know, the baked goods are worth the drive all on their own.

To prepare the rolls:
In a medium saucepan, scald the milk and add ¼ cup of the butter. Once the butter has melted, let the mixture cool and then add the salt and eggs. In a large bowl, mix the honey into the warm water. Sprinkle the yeast on top and let it sit until foamy.

When the milk mixture is cooled to lukewarm, add it to the yeast mixture. Add the flour 1 cup at a time until the mixture starts to pull away from the sides of the bowl. Then knead the dough on a well-floured surface until smooth and elastic.

Place the dough in a lightly greased bowl, cover with a towel, and let rise until doubled in size, about 1 hour. Punch down the dough and roll it into a large rectangle. Melt the other ¼ cup of butter and brush it onto the dough, then sprinkle with the sugar and the cinnamon. Roll the rectangle up lengthwise and pinch the edges together. Cut the roll in half and then cut each half into six slices. Carefully transfer the slices to a greased baking sheet. Let rise until doubled.

Preheat the oven to 400 degrees. Bake until golden brown, about 15 minutes. Cool and then top with icing.

To prepare the icing:
In a small bowl, mix the powdered sugar with the vanilla extract and enough milk to make it easy to drizzle.

(see photograph on page 4)

Cinnamon Rolls, p. 3

1 cup cornmeal

1 cup whole-wheat flour

½ cup unbleached white flour

⅓ cup honey or sugar

½ teaspoon salt

2 teaspoons baking powder

¼ teaspoon baking soda

2 eggs

1¾ cups buttermilk

½ cup milk

¼ cup (½ stick) butter, melted

Serves 4 to 6

Corn Cakes

CAFÉ REGIS, RED LODGE
CHEF/PROPRIETOR MARTHA A. YOUNG

Dubbed a community diner by owner Martha Young, this is a homey restaurant that reclaimed a historic local grocery store. The garden out back is a source for both lovely outdoor seating and many of the items on the menu. Young's corn cakes are one of the most requested recipes at Café Regis.

Mix all the dry ingredients together and form a volcano with a crater in the center. Into the crater, add the eggs, buttermilk, and milk. Beat outward from the center of the volcano until well blended. You want the consistency of pancake batter. Add more milk or water if needed, then add the melted butter.

Butter a hot griddle and pour the batter to slightly smaller than the cakes you want (they grow!). Flip when bubbles start to break. For a traditional taste, serve with pats of butter and pure maple syrup.

❧ *Chef's Tip: These cakes are great with all sorts of additions, sweet or savory. Try blueberries, bananas, apples, nuts, strawberries, or corn. My family's favorite combo is jalapeños and pecans. These ingredients should be added during cooking, before you flip the cakes. You can also top these corn cakes with anything or everything—peanut butter, strawberries, whipped cream, granola, or fried or poached eggs.*

Montana's most fertile agricultural region, known as the "Golden Triangle," fans out from the city of Great Falls to Havre and Shelby. This seven-county region annually produces 45 percent of the grain in the state. Montana routinely ranks among the top five states in the nation for wheat production.

Salsa

6 Roma tomatoes

1 yellow onion

1 jalapeño pepper

Juice of 1 lime

Cilantro, fresh or dried flakes

Salt and pepper

Farmer potatoes

8 medium red potatoes

2 tablespoons butter

1 garlic clove, minced

Scramble

1 yellow onion

4 jalapeño peppers

4 (4-ounce) elk sausage
    links or other sausage

1 red pepper, sliced thin

1 green pepper, sliced thin

½ cup (1 stick) butter

8 eggs

1 cup shredded pepper Jack cheese

½ cup sour cream

2 green onions, sliced thin

4 English muffins

Serves 4

Elk Sausage Scramble

RISING SUN MOTOR INN AND CABINS, GLACIER NATIONAL PARK
CHEF MICHAEL GORSKI

As a base camp for exploring Glacier National Park, this 1940s-era motel and cabin complex is perfectly positioned next to St. Mary Lake. Here's the ideal hearty breakfast to start a day up north.

To prepare the salsa:
Dice the tomatoes, onion, and jalapeño. Combine with the lime juice to taste. Add the cilantro, salt, and pepper to taste. Refrigerate for at least 1 hour (drain before serving).

To prepare the farmer potatoes:
Boil the potatoes to fork tender. Remove to cool (peel if desired). Cut into ¼-inch pieces. Melt 2 tablespoons of butter in a heavy-bottomed pan on medium-high heat. Add the potatoes and garlic; cook to golden brown (do not break apart by over-stirring).

To prepare the elk sausage with peppers and onions:
Slice the remaining yellow onion and four jalapeños into thin rings. Slice the sausage 1 inch thick and sauté with jalepeños, red and green peppers, and onions in ½ cup of butter. Cook until the internal temperature of the sausage is 165 degrees and the vegetables are tender.

To finish, scramble the eggs. Top the eggs with the sausage mixture, cheese, sour cream, and salsa, and garnish with the sliced green onions. Toast the English muffins. Plate the sausage scramble and serve with farmer potatoes on the side.

¼ cup (½ stick) margarine

2 cups sugar

4 eggs

1½ cups Karo® syrup,
    regular or lite

1 teaspoon vanilla extract

¼ teaspoon salt

1½ cups dry rolled oats

1 cup milk

1 cup sweetened, shredded coconut

1 unbaked 9-inch pie crust
    (see recipe on page 129)

Serves 6 to 8

Oatmeal Pie

YESTERDAY'S CALF-A, DELL   ❧   CHEF CONNIE JAMES

At the Calf-A, locals and travelers come for the pie. Located in a defunct one-room schoolhouse, the daily specials are scrawled on the old blackboard, handwritten in chalk. It's not uncommon to have your choice of six different kinds of pie, often still warm from the oven. This oatmeal rendition is as good for breakfast as it is for dessert.

Preheat the oven to 350 degrees. In a large bowl, blend the margarine and sugar, then add the eggs, Karo® syrup, and vanilla extract. Add the salt, then stir in the rolled oats. Gradually add the milk and coconut and mix until thoroughly blended.

Pour into an unbaked pie shell and bake for 1 hour.

FARM TO MARKET: WHEAT MONTANA

Dean Folkvord stands in a field of knee-high wheat, watching as two high-tech combines rhythmically comb out row upon row of grain. Every year during July and August, 15,000 acres of the Wheat Montana farm are harvested. Dean, his wife, Hope, and their family are the tour de force behind Wheat Montana, with three generations working in this family business that embodies the essence of farm-to-market principles.

At Wheat Montana they farm the grain, clean it, mill it, process it, bake it into bread, and sell it from their deli in Three Forks, Montana. Each day the bakery produces 25,000 loaves of bread made from organic and natural products. Wheat Montana breads are sold in seven western states; the specialty whole grains, cereals, and flour are sold nationwide.

Soufflé

12 eggs, separated

3 tablespoons sugar

3 tablespoons flour

1 tablespoon grated orange rind

Orange sauce

3 cups fresh orange juice

½ cup (1 stick) butter

Brown sugar

1 pint strawberries, sliced

Serves 8

Orange Omelet Soufflé

GIBSON MANSION BED & BREAKFAST, MISSOULA
PROPRIETORS TOM AND NANCY MALIKIE

At the Gibson Mansion, the first course of breakfast is usually served in-room, where guests luxuriate in the meticulously restored 1903 splendor of this Victorian-era home. Next stop is the sun-dappled dining room, where the flowery flavors of this breakfast soufflé mark the experience with even more elegance.

Preheat the oven to 375 degrees. Combine the egg whites and sugar in a bowl and whip until stiff. In a separate bowl, mix the egg yolks, flour, and orange rind. Gently fold the yolk mixture into the egg whites.

In a saucepan over medium heat, combine the orange juice and butter and sweeten to taste with the brown sugar. Heat the sauce until warm, then place a spoonful of the sauce into each of eight ramekins. Gently mound spoonfuls of the soufflé mixture into the ramekins.

Bake until lightly browned and set, about 10 minutes. Garnish with sliced strawberries and smother with additional orange sauce.

Pain perdu

½ cup (1 stick) butter, melted

1 baguette

3 cups grated Parmesan cheese

10 eggs

Pepper

2½ cups half-and-half

Basic Hollandaise Sauce
(see recipe on page 126)

Poached eggs

12 eggs

1 tablespoon white vinegar
(optional)

Garnish

European spring greens

Parmesan cheese, grated

Parsley, minced

Serves 6

Parmesan Pain Perdu Benedict

RISING SUN BISTRO, KALISPELL ❧ CHEF JENNIFER GRIFFITH

At Rising Sun Bistro, they serve six different kinds of eggs Benedict, including the "la tour," or tower, of croissants prepared four different ways. This special recipe is a way to dazzle your guests with your cooking ability and offer a twist to the classic brunch dish.

To prepare the pain perdu:
Preheat the oven to 400 degrees. Generously butter a loaf pan (15½ x 5½ x 4 inches).

Cut the baguette into ¼-inch slices and butter both sides of each slice. Place the slices in a layer on the bottom of the pan. Sprinkle 1 cup of grated Parmesan cheese over the baguette layer. Repeat with buttered baguette slices and Parmesan cheese until you have three layers.

Place the 10 eggs and a pinch of black pepper in a food processor and blend for approximately 3 minutes. While the food processor is running, slowly pour in the half-and-half. Continue to blend another 3 minutes.

Pour the mixture over the baguette layers, covering the layers completely (if needed, press down on the baguette slices). Let rest 5 to 10 minutes so the bread can soak up the mixture.

Bake the pain perdu in the oven until the top is golden and an inserted knife comes out clean, 30 minutes or longer.

While the pain perdu is baking, prepare the hollandaise sauce.

When the pain perdu is done, remove it from the oven and let rest for 15 minutes. Then remove the pain perdu from the loaf pan and let cool before slicing.

(continued on page 10)

To prepare the poached eggs:
While the pain perdu cools, poach the eggs. Fill a 12-inch frying pan with 1½ to 2 inches of water. Bring to a simmer; do not boil. As the water comes to temperature, crack six eggs into small cups, one egg in each cup. When small bubbles form at the bottom of the pan, the water is ready. Add 1 tablespoon of white vinegar to the water (optional, but it helps the egg whites stay together). Gently pour one egg at a time into the pan of simmering water, trying not to crowd the eggs (depending on the size of your pan, you may only be able to cook four at a time). Cook the eggs for exactly 4½ minutes, remove them with a slotted spoon, and lay them onto a paper towel on a plate to drain any excess water. Repeat the process with the remaining eggs.

Presentation:
Slice the pain perdu into 2-inch-thick pieces. Toss the European spring greens in your choice of vinaigrette *(see Broken Balsamic Vinaigrette Salad in the Salads & Sides chapter, page 39)* and place onto six plates. Lay a slice of pain perdu onto the greens on each plate. Put two poached eggs on each slice and top with hollandaise. Garnish with Parmesan and parsley.

⚘ *Chef's Tip: The pain perdu can be made a day ahead. To reheat, slice the perdu loaf, butter lightly on each side, and warm on a flat griddle or grill.*

(see photograph on page 1)

1 ¾ cups Wheat Montana
flour of your choice

3 ½ cups milk

4 eggs

½ teaspoon salt

1 cup fresh blueberries

¼ cup powdered sugar,
for dusting

Serves 6 to 8

Swedish Oven Pancakes

WHEAT MONTANA DELI, THREE FORKS

Oven pancakes are a feature of Scandinavian cooking. They offer a different texture from traditional skillet cakes, and they're perfect for busy mornings— you can attend to other chores while breakfast bakes and the wonderful aroma fills the kitchen.

Preheat the oven to 400 degrees. In a large bowl, mix the flour, milk, eggs, and salt until well moistened and blended. Butter a 9 x 13-inch pan and spread the batter into the pan. Gently place blueberries one by one into the batter, lightly pressing until they are half-submerged.

Bake for 35 to 40 minutes. Remove from the oven and immediately sprinkle powdered sugar evenly on top. Serve oven-hot with jam, cooked fruit, or maple syrup.

2 cups flour

3 tablespoons sugar

Pinch salt

3 eggs

2 cups milk

1 tablespoon rum

¼ teaspoon vanilla extract

¼ cup (½ stick) butter, melted

Vegetable oil

Makes 20 to 25 crêpes

🐾 *Chef's Tip: After you've made crêpes once, I encourage you to play with flavors. A little cinnamon or orange flower water is really good.*

Sweet Crêpes

LA CHATELAINE CHOCOLATE CO., BOZEMAN
CHOCOLATIERS WLADY GROCHOWSKI AND
SHANNON HUGHES GROCHOWSKI

Crêpes are a staple of every French household. Chocolatier Wlady Grochowski recalled this recipe from his own childhood kitchen in Paris. Bon appétit!

In a large bowl, mix the flour, sugar, and salt. Crack the eggs into a separate mixing bowl and blend with a stand mixer, electric mixer, or blender. Add the flour mixture gradually; as it thickens, add a quarter of the milk. Continue adding the remainder of the flour and milk, alternating to keep the batter from clumping. Add the rum, vanilla extract, and melted butter. Mix thoroughly, but avoid creating foam or bubbles in the batter. Cover and let the batter rest for a couple of hours at room temperature. This last step helps prevent the crêpes from sticking to the pan; if you're in a hurry, skip it, but expect loosening the crêpes from the pan to require more finesse.

To cook the crêpes, use a medium-size pan. A steel pan is preferable as it is lighter for flipping the crêpes, but any pan will do. Heat to medium heat with a splash of vegetable oil. Set an empty metal cup on the side to pour out extra oil, which will be reused throughout the process. Start by pouring half a ladle of batter into the hot pan, circling the pan to evenly spread the batter. Cook for a couple of minutes, then loosen the crêpe with a heat-safe spatula and flip; cook for another minute and remove. Add a little more oil to the pan and continue. Adjust heat and oil as needed; if the oil begins to smoke, the pan is too hot. Ideally, make all the crêpes at once, reserving them on a plate above a pot of simmering water so they stay warm and soft.

Serve with powdered sugar, jam, heavy whipping cream, various fruits, even Nutella. Spread the topping on, then roll or fold the crêpe.

½ cup olive oil

6 garlic cloves, diced

3 cups diced onion

6 tomatoes, diced, with juice

9 cups chunked roasted turkey

12 cups cooked hash browns
   or diced cooked potatoes

6 leaves fresh sage, minced

1 tablespoon fresh thyme, minced

Sea salt

1 tablespoon white pepper

4½ cups shredded
   Monterey Jack cheese

12 eggs

1 tablespoon herbs de Provence

Serves 6

Turkey Hash

LAUGHING HORSE LODGE, SWAN LAKE
CHEF KATHLEEN MOON

Corned beef, move over! This hash is packed with flavor, is lower in fat, and is guaranteed to fill up the hungriest cowboy you know. It's also a great dish for using up leftover turkey, potatoes, and vegetables.

Heat the olive oil in a 10-inch skillet, adding the garlic, onion, and tomatoes. Cook for two minutes, then add the turkey, potatoes, herbs, and salt and pepper. Cover and simmer for 4 to 6 minutes.

Remove the lid and place the shredded cheese on top of the hash, then replace the lid. When the cheese has melted, slide the hash onto a warmed plate and top with two eggs (any style). Sprinkle with fresh herbs.

8 eggs

¾ cup heavy cream

1 teaspoon salt

2 tablespoons butter

1½ cups sliced or
    chopped wild mushrooms

¾ cup fresh spinach leaves

¾ cup crumbled Amaltheia
    Organic Dairy goat cheese

Serves 8

Wild Mushroom Frittata

THE POLLARD HOTEL, RED LODGE
EXECUTIVE CHEF MELISSA DAVIS

Whenever possible, Chef Melissa incorporates local products and foraged ingredients into her recipes. She spends her time off searching the hills for wild mushrooms and looking for huckleberries when they are in season.

Preheat the oven to 350 degrees. In a small bowl, whisk together the eggs, cream, and salt. Set aside.

Heat a 10-inch oven-safe sauté pan or cast-iron pan. Melt the butter and add the mushrooms. Sauté until tender and remove from heat. Add the spinach leaves, egg mixture, and goat cheese. Swirl quickly with a fork or whisk and place the pan carefully in the oven.

Bake until the egg mixture is cooked all the way through, 20 to 25 minutes; the edges should be slightly golden brown and the center should not be jiggly. Remove from the oven and let stand for 5 minutes before serving.

Purple Gold—Huckleberries:
Perfect in desserts for their tartness, huckleberries are prized for their deep purple color, intense flavor, and wildness. They are not culti-vated domestically, but foraged in the mountains of Montana. In an abundant fruit year, the months of July and August yield gallons of berries that sell for $7 to $15 per pound. Look for roadside stands in the summer months around the Flathead Valley.

Appetizers & Snacks

Cornish Pasties, p. 21

24 dates

½ cup Spanish chorizo

¼ cup bleu cheese

3 to 4 slices of smoked
    peppered bacon

Makes 24 dates (about 6 servings)

Bacon-Wrapped Dates

WALKER'S AMERICAN GRILL AND TAPAS BAR, BILLINGS
EXECUTIVE CHEF MARLO SPRENG

Presenting every menu item with eclectic flair, Walker's has created a big-city benchmark since opening its doors in 1993. In the tapas bar, guests overlook the bustle of downtown Billings, sipping handcrafted cocktails and popping these savory dates like candy.

Preheat the oven to 450 degrees.

Slice into each date lengthwise from end to end, gently open, and (if not already pitted) remove the pit.

Mix the (raw) chorizo with the bleu cheese to make a paste. Generously stuff each date with the paste. Squeeze the dates closed around the stuffing (there should be enough stuffing that some is coming out of the sliced opening).

Lay the bacon slices out flat and roll each date up in bacon. Once the bacon begins to overlap, cut it and continue to wrap the next date. Each slice of bacon should wrap two or three dates. Push a toothpick or small skewer through each date to secure the bacon while cooking.

Arrange the wrapped dates on a baking sheet and bake 8 to 10 minutes, turning once, until bacon is crispy.

Ravioli filling

2 pounds bison short ribs

Salt and pepper

Vegetable oil

2 (12-ounce cans) Coca-Cola™

Moose Drool Barbecue Sauce

(see recipe on page 136)

Sweet corn cream sauce

1 tablespoon vegetable oil

2 cups kernel sweet corn

½ yellow onion, diced small

1 tablespoon apple cider vinegar

Salt and pepper

1 ½ cups heavy cream

Ravioli

Basic Pasta Dough
(see recipe on page 127)

Vegetable oil

Salt

Chili oil

1 cup vegetable oil

1 tablespoon red pepper flakes

½ tablespoon cayenne pepper

Barbecue Bison Short Rib Ravioli

CHICO HOT SPRINGS RESORT, PRAY
CHEF MORGAN MILTON

A favorite destination for locals and visitors, the restaurant at Chico has been serving up memorable cuisine for over a century. This original dish is layered with complex flavors that make for a decadent meal you won't soon forget.

To prepare the ravioli filling:
Preheat the oven to 325 degrees.

Heat a large cast-iron skillet over high heat, letting the pan get very hot. Season the meat with salt and pepper to taste. Add enough vegetable oil to coat the bottom of the pan and sear the ribs on all four sides. Place the seared ribs into a Dutch oven or braising pan. Pour the Coca-Cola™ over the ribs. If using a Dutch oven, return the ribs to the stove and bring to a boil. If using a braising pan, cover the ribs and braise in the oven until tender, about 2½ hours.

Remove the ribs from the pan and strain the liquid through a fine mesh strainer. Reduce the liquid by half; set aside. When the meat has cooled enough to work with, remove the bones and any fat or sinew. Pull the meat into "shreds" with a fork or your fingers; there should be no large pieces, just evenly sized shreds. Add the reduced liquid to the shredded meat and enough barbecue sauce to taste; mix with a fork, incorporating the meat and sauce.

See the Basic Pasta Dough recipe on page 127 for instructions on assembling the ravioli.

(continued on page 18)

Garnish

1 large carrot

1 tablespoon vegetable oil

1 or 2 green onions

Serves 6 (about 25 ravioli)

To prepare the sweet corn cream sauce:

In a skillet on high heat, add the oil, corn, onions, vinegar, and salt and pepper to taste and cook until the onions and corn are soft. Add the cream and continue to cook until thickened.

To cook the ravioli:

Bring a large pot of water to a boil, adding 1 teaspoon each of vegetable oil and salt per quart of water. Add ravioli to the boiling water; do not stir. Return water to a boil and cook until the texture of the pasta is to your liking, 5 to 7 minutes. Remove with a slotted spoon or pour into a strainer in the sink.

To prepare the chili oil:

In a small saucepan, bring the vegetable oil, red pepper flakes, and cayenne pepper to a simmer, then remove from heat. Allow to cool and strain through a fine mesh strainer.

To prepare the garnish:

Using a vegetable peeler, peel the carrot and then run the peeler from top to bottom to create long, thin strips. Fry the strips in hot oil until they're brown and crispy. Drain on a paper towel. Cut the green onion on the bias into small pieces.

Presentation:

Pour the sweet corn cream sauce into a large serving bowl. Place the ravioli into the cream sauce, drizzle with the chili oil, and top with the fried carrots and green onion.

❧ *Chef's Tip: This time-consuming recipe is well worth the effort, but it's best to make the barbecue sauce and the braised short ribs a day in advance.*

1 tablespoon minced shallots

1 teaspoon minced garlic

2 tablespoons butter

8 ounces chicken livers

2 ounces brandy

2 cups (4 sticks) butter, softened

Salt and pepper

Serves 8

Chicken Pâté

2ND STREET BISTRO, LIVINGSTON
CHEF/PROPRIETOR BRIAN MENGES

Chef Brian Menges generously serves this buttery, mousse-like pâté as a complimentary appetizer to greet guests at the restaurant, claiming it's just a great way to get rid of chicken livers. A staunch supporter of local producers, Menges knows this is more than just a thrifty, no-waste dish— it's an elegant and gracious way to start a fine meal.

Cook the shallots and garlic in 2 tablespoons of butter, until softened. Add the livers and sauté until lightly browned. Flambé with brandy, then remove from heat and let cool.

In a food processor, puree the cooled liver mixture. Then, in a stand mixer, whisk the liver puree and 2 cups of butter until smooth and creamy. Season generously with salt and a little pepper to taste.

To serve, use a pastry bag with a 1-inch tip to pipe the pâté on a plate or into a ramekin. Serve with a sliced baguette.

❧ *Chef's Tip: This recipe makes over a pound of pâté, but remember, it can freeze for up to 2 months. Separate the pâté into smaller portions and freeze them in individual bags. You can later thaw the amount you need and whip it again to regain the desired consistency.*

Filling

Vegetable oil

½ yellow onion, chopped fine

2 garlic cloves, minced

1 teaspoon chopped fresh rosemary

1½ pounds ground beef

1½ pounds russet potatoes,
    peeled and diced

2 cups beef stock

2 tablespoons flour

Pasty Dough

(see recipe on page 137)

Makes 12 pasties

❧ *Chef's Tip: Rules of rolling pastry dough include not overworking it. Press it slightly with your hand or rolling pin and roll, using plenty of flour, from the center to the edges. With practice you will be able to roll the dough into a rectangle not much bigger than the circles you are going to cut (this eliminates waste). You can reroll dough once using an equal amount of fresh dough. Try not to roll more than once or it gets tough, more like a cracker. This is a nice, rich dough and fairly forgiving.*

Cornish Pasties

BENNY'S BISTRO, HELENA
CHEF/PROPRIETOR MARGARET CORCORAN

A favorite on the tapas menu at this "locavore" restaurant, this classic miner's lunch gets an upscale update in this uptown jazz-filled dining room. Benny's proudly sources local producers for many ingredients, right down to the flour. This recipe features local beef and potatoes wrapped in a flaky crust.

To prepare the filling:

In a medium pan, heat a splash of oil and sauté the onion, garlic, and rosemary for about 2 minutes. Crumble the beef into the pan and brown, stirring to crumble evenly. Add the potatoes and just cover with beef stock. Simmer until the potatoes are tender and the beef is fully cooked. Mix the flour with ¼ cup of the broth from the pan. Return this to the pan and stir until thickened. Remove from heat and cool.

To prepare the pasties:

Preheat the oven to 375 degrees. On a lightly floured surface, roll the firm pasty dough to ⅛ inch thick. Cut the dough into 6- to 7-inch circles. You can trace around a saucer, or use a bowl with a fine rim. Spoon ⅓ cup of the cooled filling onto the bottom half of each circle and fold the crust over carefully. Pinch the edges with the tines of a fork and place on a baking sheet. Repeat until you've used up all the filling.

Bake until golden brown, 20 to 30 minutes. Pasties are best served with a gravy of your choice. Or, as a nod to the pioneering miners who made this "hand pie" popular, wrap your pasty in wax paper and enjoy it for a picnic lunch.

(see photograph on page 15)

Huckleberry simple syrup

2 cups water

2 cups sugar

1 cup huckleberries

Martini

2 ounces 44 North Mountain
    Huckleberry vodka

1 ounce Cointreau

1 ounce huckleberry simple syrup

Juice from ½ fresh lime
    (reserve rind)

Ice cubes

¼ cup sugar for rim of glass

Makes 1 martini

Huckleberry Martini

CARABINER LOUNGE, BIG SKY RESORT, BIG SKY
CHEF MICHAEL BOCKLEMANN

*The one and only huckleberry vodka, 44 North, is distilled in Idaho
using potatoes. It makes a fine Montana martini.*

To prepare the huckleberry simple syrup:
In a small saucepan, combine the water, sugar, and huckleberries.
Bring to a boil and simmer for 15 minutes. Refrigerate until
well chilled.

To prepare the martini:
Combine the vodka, Cointreau, huckleberry syrup, and lime
juice in a shaker over ice. Shake well.

Pour the sugar onto a small plate. Wet the rim of a martini glass
with the reserved lime rind and then gently place rim into the
sugar. Strain the chilled drink into the glass. Cheers!

1 ½ cups hot water

½ cup milk

1 egg, beaten

2 tablespoons honey

1 teaspoon sea salt

1 tablespoon active dry yeast

1 tablespoon fresh or dried
    rosemary

1 cup unbleached white flour

Whole-wheat flour to
    proper consistency

1 cup chopped Kalamata olives

Makes 1 loaf

With over sixty million acres
of land used for agriculture,
Montana's farms and ranches can
take at least some of the credit for
the state's wide-open spaces.

Kalamata Rosemary Bread

CAFÉ REGIS, RED LODGE   ❧   CHEF GARY FERGUSON

This rustic recipe is impressive for its punch of flavor and its simplicity. It's beautiful as an appetizer with cheese or to accompany a meal. Chef Ferguson is also a respected author, with notable books on Yellowstone, wolves, and the Rocky Mountains.

In a large bowl, combine the water, milk, egg, honey, and salt. As the ingredients mix, their temperatures will even out to about body temperature. Add the yeast and rosemary. Continue to mix, stirring in the white flour and gradually adding the whole-wheat flour until the dough is homogeneous and neither sticky nor dry. Add the Kalamata olives and mix well. Let the dough rise in the bowl for 20 minutes.

Remove the dough from the bowl and knead well on a floured counter or bread board. Shape the dough into a loaf, place it on a baking sheet, and let it rise until the dough doubles in size, an hour or more.

Preheat the oven to 375 degrees.

Bake the loaf for 40 to 50 minutes. When done, the crust will be golden brown and the bottom will sound hollow when tapped. Cool for 15 to 20 minutes before cutting.

❧ *Chef's Tip: Create a crust to match your tastes. For a shiny, moderately chewy crust, brush the dough with a beaten egg before baking. For a crustier bread, either brush or spray with water once while baking. And for a soft, shiny crust, brush with butter when the loaf is hot right out of the oven.*

(see photograph on page 24)

Kalamata Rosemary Bread, p. 23

1 tablespoon toasted sesame oil

1 tablespoon minced fresh ginger

1 tablespoon minced garlic

¼ cup minced shallots

2 tablespoons minced lemongrass

1 cup sliced shiitake mushrooms

10 pounds Manila or butter clams
    (roughly ¾ pound per person)

1 tablespoon white wine

1 cup julienned carrots

1 cup julienned snow peas

½ cup rough-chopped
    green onions

3 tablespoons chopped
    fresh cilantro

3 tablespoons chiffonade
    of fresh basil *(see Chef's Tip
    on page 2)*

3 tablespoons chiffonade
    of fresh mint *(see Chef's Tip
    on page 2)*

1 tablespoon chili oil *(see page 17)*

¼ cup fresh lemon juice

¼ cup fresh lime juice

**Serves 8 as an appetizer
or 4 as an entrée**

Manila Clams
in Asian-Style Broth

CONTINENTAL DIVIDE RESTAURANT & BISTRO, ENNIS
CHEF/PROPRIETOR ERIC TRAPP

*After decades of serving clams and mussels in traditional butter/garlic/
white wine/parsley/cream preparations, the Continental Divide decided to
offer this lighter, more colorful, fresh, and aromatic presentation as a house
appetizer. Serve over udon noodles or keep it simple with just the clams.*

Place a tablespoon of sesame oil in a warm sauté pan large enough
to hold the clams in no more than two layers. Add the aromatics
(ginger, garlic, shallots, and lemongrass) and mushrooms. Increase
heat to high and swirl around the pan. Before the garlic begins to
burn, add the clams and white wine, then cover.

When the clams begin to open, discard any that do not open and
add all the vegetables and herbs. Use a large spoon to toss well, then
cover just long enough to slightly soften the carrots and peas, 1 to 2
minutes. Season the clams to taste with the chili oil and lemon and
lime juices. Toss well again, serve in bowls, and garnish with cilantro,
basil, and mint.

7 to 8 (21 to 25 per pound)
    shrimp per person,
    shells cut but intact

1 cup (2 sticks) butter

1 cup extra virgin olive oil

4 bay leaves

½ cup chopped garlic,
    or 3 tablespoons
    granulated garlic

¼ cup crumbled rosemary

¼ cup fresh oregano

¼ cup fresh basil

¼ teaspoon cayenne pepper

1 tablespoon coarsely ground
    black pepper

2 tablespoons lemon juice

2 tablespoons Worcestershire sauce

Salt

Serves 8 as an appetizer
or 4 as an entrée

Mint-Style Barbecue Shrimp

THE MINT BAR AND CAFE, BELGRADE
CHEF/PROPRIETOR JAY BENTLEY

This barbecue shrimp really isn't barbecued, but baked. For some reason (known only to its inventor), it was named that way by the New Orleans place where it was first served, Pascal's Manale restaurant on Napoleon Avenue in uptown New Orleans. This New Orleans–inspired recipe has been on the menu at The Mint ever since it reopened in 1995. (Published with permission from Open Range: Steaks, Chops, and More from Big Sky Country *by Jay Bentley and Patrick Dillon, 2012.)*

To prepare the shrimp, use scissors to cut down along the top of the shell and devein, but leave the shells on. Cooking the shrimp in the shell enhances the flavor of the sauce and makes them easier to eat.

Preheat the oven to 450 degrees.

In a large sauté pan or oven-safe dish, melt the butter and oil over medium-high heat, then add all the ingredients *except the shrimp* and bring to a boil. Turn the heat down and simmer for 10 minutes, stirring occasionally. Turn off the heat and let the mixture stand until it reaches room temperature, 30 minutes or so. Mix in the shrimp, tossing well, and cook over medium heat until they begin to turn slightly pink. Remove from heat.

Place the pan in the preheated oven for 10 to 15 minutes; be careful not to overcook. Ladle the shrimp and sauce into bowls, being sure to include the bits of herbs and spices that have settled on the bottom, and serve hot with plenty of French bread for dipping. If cooked in an oven-safe dish, you can serve "family style" in the center of the table for everyone to share. Start peeling and eating!

❧ *Chef's Tip: This dish is best with authentic American shrimp from the Gulf of Mexico, particularly those with the heads still on. Head-on shrimp impart much more flavor to the sauce.*

Dough

1 cup (2 sticks) butter, chilled and cut into cubes

1 ½ cups flour

½ cup polenta

1 teaspoon salt

1 cold egg

1 cup ice water

Filling

2 cups cooked pheasant (or chicken) meat, chopped fine

½ cup chopped onion, sautéed

½ cup chopped red pepper, sautéed

2 teaspoons ground cumin

1 tablespoon chopped fresh cilantro

1 tablespoon chipotle Tabasco

1 cup shredded Cheddar cheese

Salt

Egg wash

1 egg

2 tablespoons water

Makes 2 dozen

Pheasant Empanada

THE GRAND HOTEL, BIG TIMBER ✱ CHEF AMY SMITH

As the slogan reads: "Serving Cattlemen, Cowboys, Sheepherders and Travelers Since 1890." This historic hotel is a local icon. It was restored in the 1990s by chef and current owner Larry Edwards. He's handed the kitchen reins to Chef Smith, and this fusion recipe is a frequent specialty on the nightly menu.

In a food processor, combine and blend the butter, flour, polenta, and salt. Place in a stand mixer bowl with a paddle attachment. Add the egg and mix, gradually adding water. Cover the mixing bowl with plastic wrap and refrigerate.

In a large bowl, combine the filling ingredients and stir until well blended.

Next, roll out the chilled dough on a lightly floured surface to ⅛ inch thickness and cut with a 5-inch biscuit cutter. Set aside the disks, reroll dough scraps, and cut into more disks. When all the dough has been cut, make an egg wash by whisking the egg and water. Brush the wash on one side of each dough disk —this will help the dough seal when you close the empanada.

Preheat the oven to 425 degrees.

Place 1 tablespoon of pheasant filling in the center of a disk, fold the dough over to make a half-circle, and pinch the edges closed to seal. Press all the air out of the empanada for a good seal. Repeat until all the disks are filled. Place the empanadas on a baking sheet and bake until golden brown, 10 to 12 minutes.

The Grand serves its empanadas on a bed of shredded lettuce and topped with mango salsa.

Beurre blanc

½ cup cava or inexpensive
    sparkling wine

1 tablespoon finely chopped shallots

1 bay leaf

1½ tablespoons heavy cream

1 cup (2 sticks) butter,
    cut into small cubes

4 tomatoes, peeled, seeded,
    and chopped

1 bulb fennel, thinly sliced or shaved

Kosher salt and black pepper

Juice from ½ lemon

Salmon cakes

2 pounds poached salmon

1 yellow onion, diced small

2 ribs celery, diced small

1 green bell pepper, diced small

1 bunch green onions,
    finely chopped

1 tablespoon finely chopped
    flat-leaf parsley

Juice from ½ lemon

¾ cup heavy cream

Kosher salt and black pepper

Creole seasoning (such as
    Prudhomme's Seafood Magic®
    or Zatarain's)

1 to 2 tablespoons butter

Poached Salmon Cakes with Tomato-Fennel Beurre Blanc

CAFÉ KANDAHAR, WHITEFISH MOUNTAIN RESORT
CHEF/PROPRIETOR ANDY BLANTON

A cornerstone of Whitefish dining for the last twenty-eight years, Café Kandahar is located inside Kandahar Lodge, in the heart of Whitefish Mountain Ski and Summer Resort. Honoring ties to the Northwest, this salmon preparation reflects the creative cuisine offered in the dining room, where vintage black-and-white photographs commemorate the beginning years of Whitefish Mountain's first proprietors and skiing legends from the 1950s.

To prepare the beurre blanc:
Pour the cava or sparkling wine into a heavy-bottomed saucepan, such as stainless steel or nonreactive aluminum, along with the shallots and bay leaf. Allow the liquid to reduce over medium heat until almost evaporated. Be sure to keep a close eye so the cava doesn't burn or caramelize, as that would change the flavor of the sauce.

Once the cava has almost completely evaporated, add the heavy cream. Using a whisk, stir the cream over medium heat until combined. Allow the cream to come to a boil and reduce slightly. Turn the heat down to low and begin to stir in the cubes of butter, one at a time, using the whisk, until evenly combined. Gently stir in the tomatoes and fennel and bring to a simmer. Season with the kosher salt, black pepper, and lemon juice. Set aside and keep in a warm but not hot place, such as a shelf above the stove.

To prepare the salmon cakes:
Combine the poached salmon, yellow onion, celery, bell pepper, green onions, parsley, and lemon juice in a large bowl. Mix well, using your hands or a wooden spoon. The salmon should be shredded with your fingers or whatever utensil you are using to mix the ingredients.

Garnish

Flour

¼ cup capers

3 ounces arugula

Serves 8 as an appetizer
or 4 as an entrée

While you are mixing the cakes, pour the heavy cream into a sauce-pan and reduce the liquid by two-thirds, or until the cream measures approximately ¼ cup and is thick and opaque. Add the reduced cream to the salmon mixture, along with the kosher salt, black pepper, and Creole seasoning to taste.

Form small patties with the salmon mixture and sear them in a buttered nonstick pan over medium-high heat until browned evenly on both sides, about 3 minutes per side. Be careful not to burn the cakes—brown is perfect, black is burnt.

To prepare the garnish:
In the same pan as the cakes, as soon as the cakes are finished but while the pan is still hot, sprinkle a few pinches of flour on the capers and sauté until they just begin to turn brown and crispy.

Serve the cooked cakes over arugula, ladle the beurre blanc over the top, and sprinkle the capers as a garnish. Enjoy!

❧ *Chef's Tip: When seasoning "to taste," a good rule of thumb is 1 teaspoon of kosher salt, ¼ teaspoon of black pepper, and ½ teaspoon of Creole seasoning per pound of salmon.*

ARTISANAL CHEESE: AMALTHEIA ORGANIC DAIRY

The pastoral setting of Amaltheia Organic Dairy beneath the Bridger Mountains belies the hectic schedule of farm life. Melvyn and Sue Brown started with 90 goats in 2002. More than a decade later they've grown to a full-fledged artisanal cheese operation with 280 goats producing 150 gallons of goat milk each day.

Amaltheia produces small-batch chèvre, feta, and ricotta cheeses, as well as flavored chèvres, such as roasted garlic and chive, spiced pepper, perigord black truffle, and sun-dried tomato. Making one pound of goat cheese takes five pounds of goat milk and a lot of hands-on attention—the chèvre alone takes three days to make. Amaltheia Dairy sells seventeen different products and has the capacity to produce 2,000 pounds of goat cheese per week. In Greek mythology, Amaltheia was the goat that nursed Zeus.

Passion fruit caviar

2 cups tapioca pearls

4 cups water

2 cups passion fruit puree
   (see Chef's Tip)

1 tablespoon sugar

2 cups water

Makes 5 cups

Grape confiture

1 pound black (Concord) grapes

½ cup sugar

2 to 4 tablespoons water (if needed)

Makes 3 cups

Brie

1 tablespoon crushed
   pink peppercorns

3 ounces (6 tablespoons) Brie

10 crackers of your choice

Serves 6 to 8

❧ *Chef's Tip: Passion fruit puree is
a sweet-tart tropical fruit flavoring.
It is available in the frozen food
section of some grocery stores or
through online retailers. Substitutes
for this exotic ingredient include
lemon or lime concentrate. Or, for
a color similar to the passion fruit,
use a raspberry puree.*

Roasted Brie

PEAKS RESTAURANT, BIG SKY RESORT, BIG SKY
CHEF MICHAEL BOCKLEMANN

*With the best view of Big Sky Resort's base area at the Summit Hotel, this
restaurant is an upscale answer to mountain cuisine. Serving a diverse clientele,
the Peaks boasts an award-winning wine list and elegant, eclectic menu
offerings, including this tropical twist on a classic cheese appetizer.*

To prepare the passion fruit caviar:
In a medium saucepan, cover the tapioca pearls with water and
bring to a boil, stirring constantly, about 15 minutes. In a large
bowl, combine the passion fruit puree, sugar, and water. Stir the
tapioca into the mixture and refrigerate overnight. Strain off any
liquid and reserve. If there is leftover puree, it can be refrigerated
for up to a week.

To prepare the grape confiture:
Place the grapes in a heavy-bottomed pot. Bring to medium heat
and cook until the skins start to burst. Sprinkle with sugar. If there
is not enough juice to dissolve the sugar, add water. Simmer at
medium heat until all the grapes have burst their skins, stirring
frequently. Cool and refrigerate.

To prepare the Brie:
Dust pink peppercorns over one edge of the Brie. Place the Brie on
an oven-safe plate in a 350-degree oven until the Brie just starts to
soften, about 3 minutes. Alternatively, soften in a microwave for
15 to 20 seconds.

Presentation:
To serve, arrange the crackers against the Brie, shingling forward.
Place about ¼ cup of the grapes in a pile opposite the crackers, and
drizzle some of the syrup around the plate. Place a tablespoon of
the caviar in front of the crackers and serve.

8 thick-sliced strips bacon
or 4 extra-thick slices
cottage bacon

½ cup (1 stick) butter,
room temperature

3 tablespoons fresh rosemary
(dried will work too)

1 garlic clove, peeled and minced

7 ounces of your favorite
made-in-Montana smoked
cheese, grated

3 cups flour

4 heaping tablespoons
baking powder

1 teaspoon salt

1 ¼ cups Missoula Draught Works
Gwin Du stout beer or your
favorite Montana stout or
homebrew

2 bell peppers in the color
combination of your choice

Serves 8

Stout Beer Scone

KAFÉ UTZA, MILES CITY ❧ CHEF KARA BROWNING

The finest and only Basque coffee shop in Montana serves food prepared with love and care. Snacking on thick strips of cottage bacon, feasting on a cheese and flatbread assortment, and sipping on a stout microbrew with Southern company inspired this particular scone. Combine beer, bacon, butter, and smoked cheese and this becomes a not-so-ordinary English scone. The following recipe calls for all-Montana ingredients.

Preheat the oven to 350 degrees.

Cook the bacon until crisp in a skillet or in the oven while it preheats. Let cool and chop.

In a food processor or electric stand mixer, combine the bacon, butter, 2 tablespoons of chopped rosemary, minced garlic, and roughly 4 ounces of the grated cheese and blend for 30 seconds. Add the flour, baking powder, and salt and slowly add the beer while blending until the ingredients just bind, another 40 seconds. Be careful not to over-mix or the scones will lose their tender consistency. Pour the mixture into the center of a greased 13 x 18-inch baking sheet. Sprinkle the mound with flour and press into an 11 x 13-inch oval. Sprinkle the remaining cheese evenly on the scone. Seed the bell peppers and slice into rings. Arrange the pepper rings in a pattern of your choice on top of the cheese. Sprinkle the remaining rosemary over the peppers and add the Love! Bake for 25 minutes. Slice into eight pieces and serve warm.

1 pint fresh strawberries,
   leaves removed

¼ cup minced fresh basil leaves

64 ounces seltzer water or
   sparkling mineral water

Serves 4 to 6

Strawberry Basil Soda

GIL'S GOODS, LIVINGSTON & PROPRIETOR BRIAN MENGES

*This refreshing, handcrafted soda is the perfect quencher on a hot day.
One sip equals pure summer.*

Trim the leaves off the strawberries and place in a bowl. Muddle
the fruit with a mortar and pestle or simply with a fork. In a pitcher,
combine the basil and seltzer or mineral water. Add the strawberries
and stir thoroughly. Prepare four tall glasses with ice and pour the
soda equally into each.

Trout

2 tablespoons flour

1 teaspoon salt

1 teaspoon pepper

1 teaspoon paprika

1 tablespoon chopped fresh parsley

1 tablespoon extra virgin olive oil

1 (8- to 10-ounce) head-on,
   whole, cleaned rainbow trout
   (see Chef's Tip)

Meunière sauce

1 teaspoon capers

1 shallot, sliced thin

¼ cup white wine

1 tablespoon butter

Garden greens

3 lemon slices

2 tablespoons (1 ounce)
   sliced pickled ginger

Serves 8

Trout Meunière

MANY GLACIER HOTEL, GLACIER NATIONAL PARK
EXECUTIVE CHEF MICHAEL GORSKI

Enjoyed over the campfire or in an elegant restaurant, this simple trout preparation is a classic meal in Glacier National Park and throughout Montana. It's a reflection of place, and when prepared with a light hand (be careful not to overcook when frying!), the delicate, flaky flesh is unforgettable.

To prepare the trout:
Combine the flour, salt, pepper, paprika, and half of the parsley in a shallow bowl. Line a plate with paper towels (for draining the fish after sautéing). Heat a sauté pan on medium-high heat and add the olive oil. As the oil warms, dust the flesh side of the trout in the flour mixture. Gently shake the trout by its tail to remove the excess. Place the trout in the oil flesh side down. Sauté for 3 minutes, then flip. Sauté for another 3 minutes, then lay the trout on the prepared plate to drain excess oil.

To prepare the meunière sauce:
In the same pan, add the capers and shallot slices and sauté for 2 minutes. Deglaze with the wine, then add the butter and remaining parsley; stir to combine.

Plate the trout on a platter of garden-fresh greens. Top with lemon slices, meunière sauce, and pickled ginger. Serve with slices of bread as an appetizer, or, as an entrée, prepare the recipe according to the number of guests (one trout is one entrée serving).

❧ *Chef's Tip: If you aren't cooking your own "catch of the day," ask your local grocery if they carry fresh trout or try www.pikeplacefish.com, a reliable fresh fish source in Seattle dedicated to selling sustainably caught fish that ships overnight in the contiguous United States.*

Salads & Sides

Purple Barley Stuffed Squash, p. 46

Dressing

2 tablespoons fresh lemon juice

3 tablespoons sugar

¼ cup vegetable oil

5 tablespoons rice wine vinegar

1 teaspoon grated fresh ginger

1 teaspoon salt

Salad

1 pound chicken breast,
   cooked and shredded

½ head green cabbage, shredded

1 cucumber, peeled, halved,
   and sliced

2 carrots, julienned

4 green onions, cut on the bias

1 orange, segments
   cut from membrane

½ cup sliced almonds, toasted

Serves 4 to 6

Asian Chicken Salad

PARK AVENUE BAKERY, HELENA   &   CHEF KATHERINE BALLEIN

Known for European-inspired breads and pastries, this longtime Helena establishment is also a cozy lunch spot with fresh, original salads, soups, and sandwiches. Supporting local farmers, Park Avenue uses Hutterite chicken for this salad.

To prepare the dressing:
Combine all the ingredients for the dressing and whisk until emulsified.

Soak the chicken in one-quarter of the dressing for 2 to 3 hours, then sauté until tender.

To prepare the salad:
Toss the cabbage, cucumbers, carrots, green onions, and orange segments with the remainder of the dressing. Add the marinated shredded chicken. Top with almonds.

1 small green cabbage

6 cups water

1 cup sugar

1 cup apple cider vinegar

1 bay leaf

1 garlic clove, peeled and chopped

1 bunch fresh thyme, chopped

Serves 6

Braised Cabbage

LONE MOUNTAIN RANCH, BIG SKY ❧ CHEF SCOTTIE BURTON

Serve with Montana Rainbow Trout (see recipe in the Main Courses chapter, page 86).

Preheat the oven to 400 degrees.

Trim the loose leaves off the cabbage, then cut in half. Cut those halves into thirds, so that you have six cabbage wedges. Place these in a deep-sided baking dish and set aside. Fill a large saucepan with 6 cups of water and add the sugar, apple cider vinegar, bay leaf, garlic, and thyme and bring to a boil for about 3 minutes. Pour the hot liquid over the cabbage wedges, cover with aluminum foil, and place in the oven until just tender, about 30 minutes. Use a slotted spoon to remove the cabbage wedges and serve.

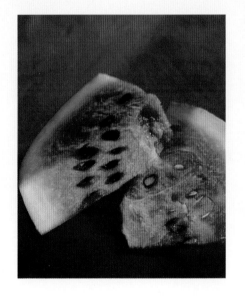

A SIGN OF SUMMER: DIXON MELONS

Like most farmers, Harley Hettick relies on the weather. But with a sensitive crop like high-country melons, the weather is an even bigger factor. An un-expected frost can wipe out the entire crop overnight, a hailstorm can dent the melons, and heavy rains can mean no melons at all during the short growing season. In their twenty-five years of farming, the Hetticks have endured many trials on their farm in tiny Dixon. Each year they sow some 34,000 plants spread out over twenty acres in Sanders County.

Folks wait all year for Dixon melons to show up at grocery stores and farmers' markets. The sweet scents of ripe muskmelon, cantaloupe, water-melon, and honeydew waft through the air on the warm summer breeze, and one bite marks the best time of year. To celebrate the harvest, the Hettick family invites the community to Dixon Melon Days each August for farm tours and games.

Dressing

½ cup minced shallots

2 tablespoons chopped fresh thyme

¼ cup whole-grain mustard

2 tablespoons sugar in the raw

¾ cup aged balsamic vinegar

1 tablespoon freshly
 ground black pepper

1 cup blended oil (a canola/olive
 blend will do nicely)

Makes 2 cups

Salad

2 cups garden greens

1 cup fresh basil

1 cup grape or cherry tomatoes

¼ cup Kalamata olives, pitted

¼ cup Amaltheia Organic Dairy
 goat cheese

1 cup radishes, sliced

Chive blossoms for garnish

Serves 8 to 12

Broken Balsamic Vinaigrette Salad

MONTANA ALEWORKS, BOZEMAN   ∽   CHEF ROTH JORDAN

Honoring the local and sustainable food movement, the seasonally changing menu at Montana Aleworks is peppered with the names of Montana farmers and ranchers. Specifically, Gallatin Valley Botanical provides local greens, herbs, and vegetables throughout the year.

To prepare the dressing:
Whisk all the ingredients (except oil) together in a mixing bowl. Slowly whisk in the oil, but do not emulsify; this is a "broken" vinaigrette. Refrigerate for up to 1 week.

To prepare the salad:
The base ingredients for this salad are fresh local greens, basil, grape or cherry tomatoes, Kalamata olives, and Amaltheia goat cheese. In a large salad bowl, toss the greens with the vegetables and dressing. Top with the goat cheese and olives, and garnish with radishes and chive blossoms.

∽ ***Chef's Tip:*** *Additional ingredients can vary depending on what your local farmers have available. Favorites include roasted beets, parsnips, herbs, sorrel, and edible flowers. The season dictates the salad.*

2 cups Israeli couscous

⅛ cup chopped fresh parsley

¼ cup chopped Kalamata olives

¼ cup crumbled feta cheese

½ cup diced artichoke hearts

½ cup chopped marinated
    mushrooms

4 whole garlic cloves

2 roasted red peppers, diced

2 tablespoons fresh lemon juice

¼ cup roasted garlic oil

Serves 8 to 10

Chilled Couscous Salad

CHICO HOT SPRINGS RESORT, PRAY CHEF MORGAN MILTON

This versatile salad is made from Israeli couscous, the grain that resembles pasta in form and texture but is much healthier. It can be paired with nearly any fish or chicken, or even with other salads.

Cook the couscous in boiling water like pasta. Cook until soft, drain, and then cool under cold water. It is finished when the beads have a soft, pasta–like consistency.

Combine the parsley, Kalamata olives, feta cheese, artichoke hearts, marinated mushrooms, whole garlic cloves, and roasted red peppers; mix in the couscous.

Make a simple dressing by mixing the lemon juice and roasted garlic oil. Stir the dressing into the couscous and refrigerate. Serve chilled.

THE CHERRY ON TOP: THE ORCHARD AT FLATHEAD LAKE

In Montana, cherry season lasts four fleeting weeks beginning in mid-July along the shores of Flathead Lake. If your timing is just right, you can catch the brief but glorious harvest from roadside stands, at farmers' markets, and in grocery stores statewide. The Orchard at Flathead Lake was started in 1976 by Ray and Carol Johnson. With 500 trees on the eastern shore, the orchard can produce more than 30,000 pounds of organic Rainier and dark sweet cherries. Today, their legacy continues to grow through their children— Bob, Bill, Roy, Terry, Shana, and Gary—who have expanded the orchard with other fruit trees and cherry products.

6 tablespoons extra virgin olive oil

1 large yellow onion,
    diced medium

1 tablespoon white wine

20 fingerling or 10 Yukon
    gold potatoes, quartered

3 tablespoons butter

2 tablespoons chopped fresh chives

1 teaspoon chopped fresh thyme

Salt and pepper

Serves 8

Agriculture remains Montana's
number one industry and is the
financial engine that drives the
state's economy, bringing in
$2 billion in annual revenue.

Fingerling Potatoes
with Caramelized Onions

MOUNTAIN SKY GUEST RANCH, EMIGRANT
CHEF BRIAN BIELEN

*Pair with Grilled Rack of Lamb with Chimmichurri Sauce (see recipe
in the Main Courses chapter, page 78).*

Heat the oven to 350 degrees.

To caramelize the onion, heat 3 tablespoons of olive oil in a pan
on medium-high heat. Toss the onions in the oil to coat and brown,
stirring occasionally. When the onions are browned on all sides,
deglaze by adding the white wine. Stir until the wine evaporates.
Remove the pan from heat and set aside.

In a mixing bowl, toss the potatoes in 3 tablespoons of olive oil,
then spread them in a single layer on a sheet pan. Bake for 25 minutes
or until tender. Remove from the oven and, as soon as possible, rough
chop—they need to stay hot. Gently fold in the butter, herbs, and
onions; season with salt and pepper to taste.

6 cups water

2 cups hulless barley

¼ cup red wine vinegar

2 cups cherry tomatoes, quartered

½ cup chopped black olives

¼ cup minced fresh parsley

1 garlic clove, minced

¼ cup crumbled feta cheese

2 tablespoons extra virgin olive oil

Salt and pepper

Serves 12

Greek Barley Salad

FARM-TO-TABLE STORE, GLENDIVE
CHEF GARTH CLINGINGSMITH

The Farm-to-Table Store in Glendive is the headquarters of Western Trails Food. It's more than a business; it's a local food movement propelled by a group of volunteers who range from farmers to foodies to chefs. The dedicated group processes hulless barley and dry beans grown throughout eastern Montana into soup mixes, barley flour, and flakes, as well as pancake and bread mixes. Look for Western Trails Food products in health food outlets, gift shops, and grocery stores from Libby to Baker. This recipe gets rave reviews from fans who've tried the hulless barley.

In a large pot, bring 6 cups of water to a boil, add the barley, and boil for 5 minutes. Remove from heat and drain off excess water. Add the vinegar and put a lid on the pot. Let the barley stand for at least an hour until tender (it will expand to about 5 cups).

When the barley is ready, add the tomatoes, black olives, parsley, garlic, feta cheese, olive oil, and salt and pepper. Toss well and serve cold or at room temperature.

Homemade Mozzarella and Garden Tomatoes, p. 44

6 to 8 cups hot water

3 (8-ounce) packs Lifeline Dairy
    Organic Plain Cheese Curds

2 to 3 large tomatoes

16 fresh basil leaves

Extra virgin olive oil and
    balsamic vinegar,
    for drizzling

Salt and pepper

Serves 8

*❧ Chef's Tip: The cooled whey water
can be set aside and used to cook
pasta or rice, especially handy if you
are making your mozzarella for a
garnish on a pasta dish.*

Homemade Mozzarella and Garden Tomatoes

CAFÉ DECAMP, BILLINGS   ❧   CHEF/PROPRIETOR JASON DECAMP

The indisputably creative and original-thinking chef at this cutting-edge eatery calls this recipe "cheater's mozzarella." Inspired by the flavor and texture of traditional buffalo mozzarella, Chef DeCamp found a way to reconstitute cultured cheese curds into a delectable form with a mouth-watering texture that he uses to accent a number of dishes in his restaurant.

Bring the hot water to a boil, then let rest for at least 8 minutes. Place the curds in a wide mixing bowl, breaking them into individual pieces. Add enough hot water to cover the curds. Begin working the curds by hand, squeezing them into each other in the water until a mass forms. Look for unmelted curds and squeeze them into the mixture as you pull and press the rest of the mass.

The water will quickly cool and cloud with whey. Once it cools and no longer aids in melting the curds, carefully pour it out without losing any cheese. Add more hot water and continue to knead until your curds are completely homogeneous and elastic. Be patient and thorough in kneading the curds. You may need to repeat the whey strain and add more hot water to achieve the desired consistency. The process will make two balls of "cheater mozzarella."

Presentation:
To serve, slice the cheater mozzarella and tomatoes (try some heirloom varieties from the local farmer's market) into ½-inch pieces. Lay the tomatoes on a platter, top with two basil leaves, and finish with the cheese slices, as in an Italian-style Caprese salad. Finely chop the remaining basil and sprinkle over the platter evenly, then drizzle with olive oil and balsamic vinegar. Salt and pepper to taste.

(see photograph on page 43)

1 cup jasmine rice

1 cup red rice

1 cup wild rice

3 cups water for each cup rice

3 tablespoons butter

Kosher salt

Serves 8

Farm and ranch vacations are a unique way to see Montana's vast open spaces. With the trend of diversifying agricultural practices, several operations open their homes and ranches for guests to experience a time-honored lifestyle in the West. Whether it's a cattle drive through the mountains or relaxing at the homestead, a visit to a working farm or ranch is a great way to gain new skills and enjoy some authentic meals. It may even change the way you look at the world.

Layered Rice

CONTINENTAL DIVIDE RESTAURANT & BISTRO, ENNIS
CHEF/PROPRIETOR ERIC TRAPP

Serve this rice dish with Macadamia-Crusted Fresh Wild Walleye (see recipe in the Main Courses chapter, page 81).

Cook the three rices separately according to directions (1 cup rice to 2 cups water is the general ratio but some rices need more water). To showcase the natural flavors, do not use stock—just water. Remember to let the rice rest for at least 10 minutes after cooking. We are looking for sticky rice. Finish each pot of rice with 1 tablespoon of butter and salt to taste.

Presentation:
Lightly spray eight espresso cups or ramekins with cooking spray. At a steep angle, press in layers of rice one color at a time until the cups are full. Cover with plastic wrap and put in a warm (180- to 200-degree) oven until service, or reheat in a microwave at service. To unmold, place a cup upside down on a plate and tap lightly.

8 cups vegetable broth

2 cups Purple Prairie Barley
    from Timeless Seeds
    (see Sources on page 143)

4 acorn or other small
    winter squash

2 tablespoons extra virgin olive oil

½ cup dried cranberries

½ cup golden raisins

1 cup walnuts

1 teaspoon salt

1 teaspoon pepper

Serves 8

Purple Barley Stuffed Squash

TIMELESS SEEDS, CONRAD

This is a very simple and tasty dish, with a great autumn table presentation. Purple Prairie Barley is grown in Montana's own "golden triangle."

In a large saucepan, bring the vegetable broth to a boil and add the Purple Prairie Barley. Cover, reduce to simmer, and cook until the broth is absorbed and the barley is tender, about 1 hour.

While the barley is cooking, split the squash in half, scoop out the seeds, and coat the flesh with olive oil. Place the squash cut side down in a baking dish. Bake at 350 degrees until just tender, about 15 minutes.

When the barley is tender, remove from heat. Mix in the cranberries, raisins, walnuts, salt, and pepper. Place a scoop into each squash half. Serve each person his or her own filled squash bowl.

(see photograph on page 35)

Pesto-mayo dressing

2 cups fresh basil

4 garlic cloves

¼ cup pine nuts

½ cup extra virgin olive oil

½ cup Parmesan cheese

2 cups mayonnaise

Salt and pepper

Salad

1 pound small red potatoes

½ red onion, diced small

1 cup cherry tomatoes, halved

Candied walnuts

2 tablespoons butter

½ cup walnut halves
    or whole pieces

1 tablespoon brown sugar

Pinch cayenne pepper

¼ cup crumbled Gorgonzola cheese

½ cup mixed greens

Serves 8

Red Potato and Walnut Salad

GLACIER PARK LODGE, EAST GLACIER PARK
EXECUTIVE CHEF MICHAEL GORSKI

This refreshing twist on the classic picnic side dish brings fresh flavors of garden tomatoes, salad greens, and fresh basil to the table for a memorable taste of summer with a creamy pesto accent.

To prepare the pesto-mayo dressing:
Combine the basil, garlic, and pine nuts in a food processor; pulse 3 to 4 times. Slowly add the oil while pulsing to combine. Add the cheese and pulse to blend, creating a pesto base. Mix with the mayonnaise and season to taste with salt and pepper. Cover and refrigerate for later.

To prepare the salad:
Boil the potatoes to almost fork tender. Remove to cold water to cool. When cool, cut in half. In a large bowl, combine the pesto-mayo, potatoes, onions, and tomatoes.

To prepare the candied walnuts:
Melt the butter in a pan over medium-high heat. In a bowl, combine the walnuts, sugar, and cayenne pepper. Add to the melted butter and stir until combined and the sugar coats all the nuts. Pour onto a plate and separate the nuts to cool.

Presentation:
To serve, place the mixed greens on individual plates or on a large platter for family-style, top with the potato mixture, and garnish with candied walnuts and Gorgonzola cheese crumbles.

8 large beets, peeled and
   diced into 1-inch squares

2 tablespoons extra virgin olive oil

½ cup Black Pepper Vinaigrette
   (see recipe on page 128)

2 cups crumbled Gorgonzola cheese

2 Granny Smith apples,
   quartered and julienned

1 cup roasted pistachios, chopped

1 bunch watercress, for garnish

Serves 8

Farm to Market: With close to
seventy farmers' markets throughout the state, from Absarokee
to Whitefish and everywhere in
between, it's easy to purchase
goods directly from the producers.
Each market is different, depending
on the region and month, but it's
possible to purchase locally grown
products ranging from apples to
wool. Most markets are held from
June through September.

Roasted Beet Salad
with Black Pepper Vinaigrette

PARADISE VALLEY GRILL, LIVINGSTON   ❧   CHEF JOSH PASTRAMA

*Chef Pastrama opened his restaurant with a vision: to incorporate Napa
Valley cuisine with Montana's sustainable food products in a one-of-a-
kind dining experience. Close relationships with local farmers and ranchers
ensure not only the freshest ingredients, but also a culinary experience that
celebrates Montana's bounty.*

Preheat the oven to 350 degrees. Toss the diced beets with olive oil
and place on a baking sheet or roasting pan. Roast in the oven until
fork-tender, 20 to 30 minutes. Remove to a separate plate and let
cool in the refrigerator (this can be done a day ahead if necessary).

Place the diced beets into a small bowl and toss with ½ cup of
vinaigrette. On eight medium-size plates, place equal amounts of
dressed beets in the center of each plate, then ring with the cheese,
apples, and pistachios. Finish by garnishing with the watercress
on top and a little drizzle of vinaigrette around each plate.

1 cup (2 sticks) butter

4 tablespoons extra virgin olive oil

6 garlic cloves

½ cup dry white wine

8 large portobello mushrooms,
      or 8 cups other firm mushrooms

2 cups coarsely chopped fresh sage

Dash sea salt

½ teaspoon white pepper

½ cup crumbled Gorgonzola cheese

1 cup coarse bread crumbs
      (dark preferred)

8 sprigs fresh sage, for garnish

Serves 8

Sautéed Portobellos
in Sage and Gorgonzola

LAUGHING HORSE LODGE, SWAN LAKE
CHEF KATHLEEN MOON

Warning! This dish is a celebration of calories! Sinfully delicious and absolutely forbidden on any sane diet, it's a delectable side dish with a good Montana steak.

In a 10-inch sauté pan, heat the butter and olive oil. Add the garlic and cook until soft but not golden. Add the wine and cook until it reduces, 2 to 3 minutes. Add the mushrooms and toss, coating all sides. Continue to cook on medium heat, adding the sage, salt, and pepper. When the garlic begins to brown, add the cheese and bread crumbs and toss over heat until the cheese begins to melt, about 1 minute. Top with sage sprigs. Serve hot.

1 tablespoon butter

½ sweet yellow onion,
    such as Vidalia, julienned

6 to 8 Roma tomatoes,
    sliced (4 to 5 slices each)

Salt and pepper

3 tablespoons mayonnaise

¾ cup shredded sharp white
    Cheddar cheese

¾ cup shredded mild yellow
    Cheddar cheese

3 tablespoons grated
    Parmesan cheese

1 baked 9-inch pie shell, cooled
    (see recipe on page 139)

1½ tablespoons Dijon-style mustard

1 tablespoon chopped fresh basil

Serves 6 to 8

Savory Tomato Pie

LOULA'S CAFÉ, WHITEFISH
CHEF/PROPRIETOR MARY LOU COVEY

Served at the annual Taste of Whitefish, this Southern-inspired savory pie is best made during peak tomato season, with the ripest garden-fresh ingredients.

Preheat the oven to 375 degrees. Melt 1 tablespoon of butter in a sauté pan over medium heat and brown the sweet onions. While the onions are cooking, lay the tomato slices out flat and season both sides with salt and pepper. In a bowl, combine the mayonnaise and all three cheeses.

When the onions are done, brush the bottom of the prebaked pie shell with the Dijon-style mustard. Arrange the tomatoes in layers in the pie shell. Evenly disperse the caramelized onions in with the tomatoes and then sprinkle basil on top. Spoon the mayo mixture over the tomatoes and spread to the edges so the tomatoes are covered.

Place in the oven on the middle rack and bake for 20 to 25 minutes. For added color, put the oven on broil for the last couple of minutes. Remove and let stand for 10 minutes before serving.

❧ ***Chef's Tip:*** *Do not substitute other tomatoes for the Romas; other varieties have too much water content and make the pie mushy.*

2 cups flour

7 eggs

¼ cup milk

12 cups water

Salt

8 to 10 cups ice water

2 tablespoons extra virgin olive oil

Serves 8

Spaetzle Dumplings

LONE MOUNTAIN RANCH, BIG SKY   ❧   CHEF SCOTTIE BURTON

By itself spaetzle is bland, but paired with a good sauce, it becomes a "blank canvas" for your favorite flavors. Here it's paired with Montana Rainbow Trout (see recipe in the Main Courses chapter, page 86). It's also an interesting starch alternative to pasta or potatoes.

Combine the flour, eggs, and milk in a large bowl. Mix with a wooden spoon until well combined. Cover with plastic wrap and refrigerate for at least 1 hour, or overnight.

Bring two stockpots of salted water to a boil. (Using two pots cuts the time at the stove in half.) Fill a large bowl with ice water and keep it near the stove. Take the batter out of the fridge and stir. It should be the consistency of thick pancake batter; thin with a little milk or thicken with a bit more flour as necessary. With a long spatula or knife, spread about ⅛ cup of the batter on a wooden cutting board, from the edge inward, about ¼ inch thick. Using the side of the spatula or the blade of the knife, begin pushing the ribbons of batter into the boiling water, where they will form rough-looking dumplings. When they're finished cooking, in about 2 minutes, they'll float to the top. Use a slotted spoon or strainer to remove them and slip them into the ice water. When cool, remove the dumplings, drain in a colander, and toss with a little olive oil to prevent sticking.

Reserve spaetzle in the refrigerator until you are ready to put the rest of the dish together. To serve, warm in a sauté pan over medium heat for about 8 minutes.

8 to 10 cups chicken stock

½ cup (1 stick) butter

4 shallots, finely chopped

3 cups Arborio rice

1 cup white wine

4 tablespoons assorted
    freshly chopped herbs

1 cup heavy whipping cream

1 cup grated
    Parmigiano-Reggiano cheese

White or black truffle oil

Salt and pepper

Serves 8

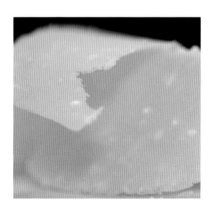

Truffle Risotto

BUCK'S T-4 LODGE, BIG SKY   ❧   CHEF CHUCK SCHOMMER

The basic risotto technique is to introduce hot stock in small amounts until the rice is tender. Italian cooks would never add cream; they would let the starches of the rice break down and make the dish creamy. To make risotto at Buck's, they add cream for extra richness with the truffle oil.

In a large stockpot, warm the chicken stock over medium–low heat. While the stock is warming, heat a heavy-bottomed sauté pan over medium heat. Add the butter and let it melt until slightly brown. Add the shallots and cook until transparent. Add the Arborio rice, stirring to coat the rice with the butter and shallots. Reduce the heat to medium–low and add just enough chicken stock to cover the rice. Simmer until the stock is absorbed, then add more hot chicken stock. Continue this process until the rice is cooked but still slightly crunchy.

To finish, add the white wine and stir until it's incorporated. Add the fresh herbs (make your own blend of flat-leaf parsley, oregano, thyme, and a dash of rosemary or sage) and heavy cream; cook the risotto until the rice is tender, adding more cream if necessary. Top with the Parmigiano-Reggiano cheese and a dash of truffle oil, and season to taste with salt and pepper. Serve immediately.

❧ *Chef's Tip: For a quicker option, par-cook the risotto a couple of days in advance. At the stage where the chicken stock has been absorbed but the rice is still crunchy, remove the rice from the pan and spread in a thin layer onto a baking sheet, then cool completely. The par-cooked rice can then be refrigerated in a lidded container for several days. When you're ready to finish the risotto, heat a heavy-bottomed sauté pan again over medium-low heat and follow the recipe instructions above.*

3 large yams, peeled and quartered

1 large Yukon gold potato,
    peeled and quartered

½ cup (1 stick) butter,
    room temperature

¼ cup brown sugar

Salt and pepper

Serves 8

Montana's farmers' markets have
grown from only five in 1990 to
more than seventy today.

Whipped Yams

PARADISE VALLEY GRILL, LIVINGSTON   ❧   CHEF JOSH PASTRAMA

*Pair this creamy side dish with Maple-Brined Pork Chops with Cranberry
Reduction (see recipe in the Main Courses chapter, page 84).*

In a medium pot, cover the yams and potato with cold water and
bring to a boil. Reduce to a simmer and cook until tender. Drain the
water and place the yams and potato in the mixing bowl of a stand
mixer or other electric mixer. Add the butter and brown sugar and
slowly whip the mixture using a whisk attachment. Once smooth,
season with salt and pepper and cover with foil in a warm oven
until ready to plate.

Soups & Stews

Steak, Lime, and Tortilla Soup, p. 65

Chili

2 pounds ground bison

1 large or 2 small onions, diced

8 garlic cloves, minced

1 (15-ounce) can tomato sauce

1 (15-ounce) can diced tomatoes

1 (16-ounce) can kidney beans

1 (16-ounce) can black beans

1 (16-ounce) can garbanzo beans

2 tablespoons chili powder

2 teaspoons crushed
    red pepper flakes

4 tablespoons ground cumin

Salt and pepper to taste

Garnish

1 to 2 avocados

1 cup sour cream

¼ cup chopped fresh cilantro

Serves 10 to 12

Bison Chili

ONYX BAR & GRILL, LEWISTOWN   ❧   CHEF GARY KUHNS

In the recently restored historic Calvert Hotel, the Onyx offers a gathering place for special occasions and weeknight respite. This chili is splendidly simple, and the end result is unforgettably delicious.

Brown the bison in a large skillet with the onions and garlic. In a 6- to 8-quart pot, bring the tomato sauce, diced tomatoes, beans, chili powder, red pepper flakes, cumin, salt, and pepper to a boil and then reduce to a simmer. Add the bison mixture and simmer on low heat for 1 hour.

To serve, garnish with thin slices of avocado, dollops of sour cream, and a sprinkle of cilantro.

½ cup diced onion

½ cup (1 stick) butter

6 tablespoons flour

1 tablespoon curry powder

6 cups fresh corn kernels,
    pulsed well in food processor

6 cups milk

2 cups heavy cream

Salt and white pepper

1 pound precooked
    Dungeness crab, shelled

4 slices cured bacon,
    cooked and crumbled

Serves 8

In 2012, Montana led the nation
in pea and lentil plantings,
accounting for more than
40 percent of the U.S. crop.

Corn and Crab Bisque

HARPER & MADISON BAKERY AND CAFÉ, BILLINGS
CHEF JOANIE SWORDS

Tucked into a well-appointed neighborhood in historic Billings, this old grocery building turned chic café and specialty market is an oasis. The menu rotates daily, and on a cold, blustery day in the city you just might find this luscious bisque.

Sauté the onion in butter. Add the flour and curry powder and cook for 2 minutes. Add the chopped corn and cook on low for 20 minutes, stirring often. Add the milk, cream, salt, and pepper and cook for another 20 minutes. Make sure all pieces of shell are removed from the crab meat, then gently stir the crab into the bisque and simmer for 5 minutes.

Serve with a sprinkle of crumbled bacon.

❧ ***Chef's Tip:*** *Canned Dungeness crab can work as a substitute for fresh.*

4 tablespoons extra virgin olive oil

1 large yellow onion, minced

3 tablespoons minced ginger root

1 teaspoon minced garlic

3 pounds carrots, peeled and diced

1 tablespoon curry paste
   or curry powder

4 cups homemade chicken stock

2 cups half-and-half

Salt and white pepper

2 teaspoons chopped fresh cilantro
   (leaves only), for garnish

Serves 8

Against all odds, Montana is home
to two vineyards that produce a
range of vintages using grapes
grown in the toughest of high-
country conditions: Ten Spoon
Vineyard and Winery near
Missoula and Mission Mountain
Winery near Dayton.

Ginger, Carrot, and Curry Soup

DISCOVERY SKI AREA, WEST OF ANACONDA
CHEF MIKE SAUER

With a delicious balance of spicy and sweet, this elegant soup is the perfect belly-warmer after a day on the slopes at "Disco," Montana's best-kept secret of a small-town ski area, where the food is just as good as the skiing.

In a medium stockpot over medium heat, add the oil, onions, and ginger root; cook, stirring occasionally, until the onions start to brown, about 7 minutes.

Add the garlic, carrots, and curry and cook for about 2 minutes. Add the chicken stock and cook until the carrots are tender, about 30 minutes.

Puree the soup in batches and return to the pot. Add the half-and-half and reheat. Add the salt and white pepper to taste and serve with a garnish of chopped cilantro on top.

2 medium acorn squash,
    quartered and seeds removed

⅓ cup extra virgin olive oil

1 teaspoon ground cinnamon

1 teaspoon chili powder

¼ teaspoon ground nutmeg

¼ teaspoon ground cloves

2 teaspoons fresh thyme

Salt and pepper

1 yellow onion, quartered

2 tablespoons chopped garlic

1 bay leaf

2 cups dry white wine

6 cups vegetable stock

¼ cup heavy cream,
    as needed for blending

Cayenne pepper

Sour cream (optional)

Honey (optional)

Serves 8

Roasted Acorn Squash Soup

THE OLD HOTEL, TWIN BRIDGES
CHEFS BILL AND PAULA KINOSHITA

Little Twin Bridges—with both the Jefferson and Ruby Rivers flowing through town—is a haven for fly-fishing anglers in the know. After a great day on the local streams, the smartest of them hit the restaurant at The Old Hotel. It's an unlikely place for two Hawaiian Island–trained chefs, but here they are. The menu changes seasonally and reflects their love of fresh ingredients, just like in this classic autumn soup.

Preheat the oven to 425 degrees. Place the squash cut–side down in a shallow roasting pan, drizzle thoroughly with olive oil, sprinkle with dry spices and thyme, and season with salt and pepper. Cover with foil and roast in the oven until the squash is fork tender, 40 to 45 minutes.

Remove the squash from the oven and allow to cool uncovered. When cool enough to handle, scrape the squash meat from the skin into a medium stockpot. Discard the skins. Add the onions, garlic, bay leaf, and any herbs and juice left in the roasting pan to the pot.

On high heat, bring to a boil. Add the wine and reduce the liquid by half. Add the vegetable stock and reduce heat to medium–low; simmer for 20 minutes. Skim any oil and impurities off the surface often. Turn off the heat and discard the bay leaf. Puree in a blender until smooth, adding cream or additional stock as necessary to achieve a smooth, creamy consistency.

Return the puree to the soup pot and reheat. Season to taste with salt, pepper, and cayenne pepper. You may want to add a dollop of sour cream and a swirl of honey on top to take the edge off the heat from the spices.

2 tablespoons butter

3 sprigs fresh rosemary

Juice from ½ lemon

1 bay leaf

2 to 3 uncooked chicken breasts
    (depending on size, need
    about 3 cups when cooked)

3 tablespoons canola oil or butter

1 cup diced carrots

2 cups diced onion

1 cup diced celery

1 tablespoon minced garlic

3 cups sliced button mushrooms

Salt and pepper

½ cup dry white wine

1 cup flour

3 cups milk

3 cups chicken broth

1 tablespoon Worcestershire sauce

¼ cup heavy cream

Serves 8 to 10

Rosemary Chicken and Mushroom Soup

LOULA'S CAFÉ, WHITEFISH

This corner café is known for more than a great slice of huckleberry-peach pie—their savory side is just as delicious.

In a medium saucepan over medium-low heat, add the butter, rosemary, lemon juice, bay leaf, and chicken and cover with a lid. Cook until the chicken is done and tender, about 8 minutes. Remove the chicken breasts and allow them to cool to the touch. Dice the chicken into bite-size pieces and set aside. Strain the cooking liquid and reserve.

In a large stockpot on medium to medium-high, combine the oil or butter, carrots, onions, celery, garlic, and mushrooms. Season with two pinches of salt and one pinch of pepper. Sauté until vegetables start to caramelize lightly, then add the white wine, stirring often, and reduce by half. Add the flour to the vegetable mixture, stirring constantly to prevent burning. When the flour has been completely incorporated, add the milk and stir continuously until the milk comes up to temperature and starts to thicken. Add 3 cups chicken broth and bring to a boil. Add the diced chicken, Worcestershire sauce, and another pinch of salt and pepper, then reduce the heat to simmer and stir occasionally.

If the soup seems too thick, add the reserved chicken stock mixture a little at a time to thin until the consistency suits you. Then add the heavy cream and simmer for 5 more minutes. Taste and adjust seasoning as desired before removing from the stove.

To serve, ladle into bowls and garnish with a sprig of fresh rosemary and a big slice of warm artisan bread.

5 large apples, such as Gala or
    Granny Smith, preferably local

1 teaspoon fennel seeds

1 teaspoon red pepper flakes

1 teaspoon ground cloves

1 cup (2 sticks) butter

1 celeriac bulb

10 parsnips

5 turnips

1 rutabaga

1 fennel bulb

10 fresh sage leaves

½ cup extra virgin olive oil

4 white onions, diced

2 leeks, diced

½ head celery, diced

2 quarts milk

2 quarts nonalcoholic apple cider

Kosher salt to taste

Serves 12

Soup of Roasted Montana Apples and Winter Root Vegetables

THE RESORT AT PAWS UP®, GREENOUGH
CHEF ADAM COOKE

Chef Cooke has a hand in leaving a lasting impression on guests who venture to find the remote Resort at Paws Up®. It's a place where wilderness and luxury meet harmoniously, and the elegant fare served in this rustic setting is one of the highlights of "roughing it" here.

Core, but do not peel, the apples and cut each into eight slices. Combine the fennel seeds, red pepper flakes, and cloves. Rub the apple slices generously with 1 stick of softened butter and coat with the spice mix. Roast on a parchment–lined baking sheet at 325 degrees for 45 minutes, allowing apples to deeply caramelize. Set aside.

While the apples are roasting, medium dice the celeriac, parsnips, turnips, rutabaga, fennel bulb, and sage leaves. Warm the ½ cup of olive oil in a large pot. Cook over medium heat until very caramelized and soft—do not be afraid to put an aggressive amount of color on the vegetables.

Add the diced onions, leeks, and celery and cook until soft. Use the moisture from the onions and celery to scrape the bits from the bottom of the pan. Add roasted apples, then the milk and cider and bring to a boil. Reduce to a simmer and cook for 45 minutes.

Using a blender, puree in batches, adding bits of butter 1 tablespoon at a time and correcting seasoning as you go, using kosher salt carefully. Strain the soup, serve, and garnish with a slice of fresh apple on each bowl.

Steak soup

8 cups water

2 tablespoons beef base

2 tablespoons apple cider vinegar

1 pound steak (rib eye or striploin)

Mirepoix

2 tablespoons extra virgin olive oil

1 tablespoon pureed garlic

¼ seeded jalapeño, diced

½ red bell pepper, chopped

½ Bermuda onion, chopped

Zest and juice from ½ lime
    (save other ½ for garnish)

1 tablespoon fresh thyme, chopped

1 celery stalk, diced

Garnish

1 large flour tortilla

Lime slices

Serves 8

Steak, Lime, and Tortilla Soup

THE WINDBAG SALOON & GRILL, HELENA
CHEF TRAVIS MCEWAN

The capital city's most iconic saloon and steak house on Last Chance Gulch is an essential stop for both its history and its killer burgers. For "lighter" fare, don't forget this tangy steak alternative.

To prepare the soup:
In a large pot, combine the water, beef base, and apple cider vinegar and bring to a simmer. Grill the steak on a charbroiler or outdoor grill, 6 minutes per side, marking once per side. Then trim the fat, dice the steak, and add to the simmering stock.

To prepare the mirepoix:
In a medium sauté pan, warm the olive oil and sauté the pureed garlic. Remove from heat and combine with the jalapeño, bell pepper, onion, lime zest and juice, thyme, and celery. Add the mirepoix to the stock and simmer for an additional 20 minutes.

To prepare the garnish:
Slice the tortilla into ¼-inch strips and fry in vegetable oil until crispy. To serve, sprinkle the tortilla strips onto the soup and garnish each bowl with a thin slice of lime.

(see photograph on page 55)

½ teaspoon dried basil

½ teaspoon dried oregano

½ teaspoon dried thyme

½ teaspoon dried rosemary

½ teaspoon peppercorns

1 bay leaf

2 cups boiling water

½ cup (1 stick) butter

1 ½ teaspoon garlic powder
 or chopped garlic

2 cups chopped onion

2 cups chopped celery

1 cup chopped carrots

¼ cup sundried tomatoes
 in olive oil

½ cup fresh basil

1 tablespoon chopped fresh parsley

¼ cup sugar

Juice from ½ lemon

¾ cup fresh tomatoes, diced, or
 1 (#10) can crushed tomatoes

Serves 8

Tomato Basil Soup

COFFEE POT BAKERY CAFÉ, FOUR CORNERS
CHEF MARCI GEHRING

From this serene roadside café and pottery studio comes food infused with care and kindness. This savory soup is the perfect repository for summer's fresh garden herbs and abundant tomatoes. It's a versatile soup that also makes a great base for a beef vegetable soup, or leftovers can be reduced and used for a rich pasta sauce.

Steep the dried herbs and bay leaf in the 2 cups of boiling water for 20 minutes, or overnight. Strain and reserve the water for the soup. Discard the herbs.

In a large stockpot, melt the butter and add the garlic, onions, celery, carrots, sundried tomatoes, and basil. Cook on medium-high heat until soft, about 45 minutes. Add 10 to 12 cups of water (including the 2 cups of reserved herb water) and bring to a boil. Strain the liquid and return it to the pot. Puree the strained vegetables in a food processor or blender until smooth. Add the puree back to the pot with the liquid. Add the parsley, sugar, lemon juice, and tomatoes. Adjust seasonings to taste and briefly bring to a boil.

Serve hot with freshly baked bread, garden salad, or—like "Mom used to do it"—with a grilled cheese sandwich.

Main Courses

Alaskan Halibut Cheeks, p. 69

Pesto

2 tablespoons fresh flat-leaf parsley, stems removed

1 tablespoon fresh basil, stems removed

¼ cup rough-chopped spring onion

3 garlic cloves

¼ cup pine nuts, toasted

½ teaspoon lemon zest

Salt and pepper

1 to 1¼ cups extra virgin olive oil

Mustard-caper butter sauce

Juice from 1 lemon

½ cup dry white wine

¼ cup heavy cream

1 cup (2 sticks) butter, cubed small

3 tablespoons whole-grain mustard

2 tablespoons capers

Salt and pepper

Alaskan Halibut Cheeks with Potato-Scallion Pesto Salad and Mustard-Caper Butter Sauce

POMPEY'S GRILL, SACAJAWEA HOTEL, THREE FORKS
CHEF MATT ISRAEL

This multi-layered dish is a sophisticated nod to pub-style fish 'n' chips. Chef Israel brings all the comfort of that classic dish and adds the refinement suitable for the elegant dining room at the iconic Sacajawea Hotel.

To prepare the pesto:
In a food processer, combine the parsley, basil, onion, garlic, pine nuts, lemon zest, and salt and pepper to taste, and pulse to break it down a bit. With the processor running, slowly add the olive oil until you reach the desired consistency—not too thick, not too thin.

To prepare the mustard-caper butter sauce:
In a small saucepan, combine the lemon juice and white wine. Cook over medium heat until the liquid is reduced to a quarter of the initial volume. Add the heavy cream and simmer the sauce base until it is reduced by three-quarters. Turn the heat down and slowly emulsify the butter into the sauce one or two cubes at a time. Watch the heat—if the sauce boils or gets too hot it will break. Whisk in the mustard and capers. Season with salt and pepper to taste.

To prepare the halibut cheeks:
With a mortar and pestle, grind the sel gris, peppercorns, garlic, smoked paprika, and onion. Trim any membrane or silver skin off the cheeks. Evenly season both sides of the halibut cheeks and dredge them in the flour, shaking off any excess.

Halibut cheeks

1 teaspoon sel gris
(coarse gray sea salt)

8 whole black peppercorns

1 teaspoon dried minced garlic

½ teaspoon smoked paprika

1 teaspoon dried minced onion

2 pounds fresh Alaskan halibut
cheeks *(see Chef's Tip)*

¼ cup flour

1 tablespoon extra virgin olive oil

2 tablespoons butter

Potato-scallion salad

2 tablespoons butter

8 red potatoes, par-cooked
and cubed

7 cups baby spinach, loosely
packed, stems removed

Salt and pepper

Serves 6 to 8

Place a large cast-iron skillet or heavy-bottomed sauté pan over medium heat; add the olive oil and butter. When the butter has melted and is starting to lightly brown, add the halibut cheeks. Sear for about 2 to 3 minutes on each side, depending on the thickness of the cheeks. Transfer to a warm plate.

To prepare the potato salad:
Using the same pan the halibut cheeks were cooked in, melt 2 tablespoons of butter and sauté the potatoes. When the potatoes are warmed through, toss with the desired amount of pesto, add the spinach and cook until just wilted. Season with salt and pepper to taste.

Presentation:
To serve, spoon the potato salad onto plates, lay the halibut on top of the potatoes, and ladle the desired amount of sauce on top of the fish.

❧ *Chef's Tip: Halibut cheeks are prized for their delicate sweet flavor, snow-white color, and firm, flaky meat. Expect six to ten cheeks per pound. They are easy to cook and should not be difficult to find locally. You can also order them through Pike Place Fish Market (see Sources on page 143), or substitute 2 pounds of fresh halibut, cut into 2-ounce fillets, sliced ½ inch thick.*

(see photograph on page 67)

Stuffing

½ pound andouille sausage

1 tablespoon extra virgin olive oil

1 cup finely diced yellow onion

3 garlic cloves, minced

½ bunch green onions,
    thinly sliced

6 tablespoons butter

1 tablespoon fresh thyme

½ cup bread crumbs

Quail

4 quail, semi-boneless

1 teaspoon Paul Prudhomme's
    Meat Magic®

Serves 4

Andouille Stuffed Quail

CAFÉ KANDAHAR, WHITEFISH   ✦   CHEF ANDY BLANTON

Small, yet flavorful, this could be served as an appetizer alone or paired with a savory dish such as Truffle Risotto (see recipe in the Salads & Sides chapter, page 53) for a main course.

To prepare the stuffing:
Cut the andouille into several pieces and pulse in a food processor until the andouille appears ground. Heat the olive oil in a large skillet over medium-high until hot. Sauté the ground andouille, stirring constantly, for approximately 45 seconds. The andouille should begin to stick to the pan and caramelize. As soon as the caramelization starts, add the yellow onions and continue to sauté over medium-high heat until the onions become translucent, approximately 3 to 4 minutes. Stir the mixture to prevent it from turning black in the pan (brown is good, black is bitter). A good wooden spoon should help.

Add the garlic and green onions and continue to sauté for another minute. Add the butter and fresh thyme. Remove from heat and stir until the butter melts. Allow the mixture to cool slightly by moving it from the skillet into a bowl, then stir the bread crumbs into the mixture and let it cool completely.

To prepare the quail:
Once the stuffing is cooled, divide it into four parts and, using a spoon or your hands, fill each quail with as much stuffing as you can.

Preheat the oven to 450 degrees.

Rub each quail with Paul Prudhomme's Meat Magic® on all sides and place in a broiling pan in the oven for about 7 to 9 minutes. The size of the quail will determine the needed cooking time.

Seasoning

4 cups finely diced yellow onion

3 tablespoons chopped fresh garlic

1 tablespoon chopped fresh basil

1½ teaspoons chopped fresh thyme

1½ teaspoons chopped
    fresh oregano

1½ teaspoons chopped fresh parsley

1 tablespoon granulated garlic

1 tablespoon onion powder

1 tablespoon pepper

¼ cup kosher salt

1 tablespoon brown sugar

½ cup your favorite steak sauce

Meatloaf

1¼ pounds ground fresh bison

1¼ pounds ground fresh beef

1¼ pounds ground fresh pork

5 eggs

3 cups panko bread crumbs

½ pound raw thin-sliced bacon

Serves 6 to 8

Bacon-Wrapped Montana Meatloaf

MONTANA ALEWORKS, BOZEMAN   ❧   CHEF ROTH JORDAN

With a menu of Montana farmers and ranchers that reads like a resource guide to local eating, this hearty recipe incorporates three different types of meat produced in-state: bison, beef, and pork. Plus, admits Chef Jordan, "Everything is better with bacon."

To prepare the seasoning:
In a small stockpot, sweat the onions until they're translucent, then add the fresh garlic and cook an additional 2 to 3 minutes. Stir in the basil, thyme, oregano, parsley, granulated garlic, onion powder, pepper, salt, brown sugar, and steak sauce. Mix well and then spread on a baking sheet to cool.

To prepare the meatloaf:
In a large mixing bowl, mix the ground bison, beef, and pork and fold in the cooled onion mixture and eggs by hand. Stir in the bread crumbs and form into a loaf. Wrap the loaf with the bacon, being sure to stretch the bacon and wrap it tightly, with pieces overlapping. Tuck the ends securely under the loaf in a bread pan. The bacon will shrink during cooking and help keep the loaf's shape.

Bake at 300 degrees until the loaf reaches an internal temperature of 155 degrees, approximately 1 hour. Slice and serve with your choice of side dishes and fresh vegetables.

(see photograph on page 72)

Bacon-Wrapped Montana Meatloaf, p. 71

4 cups chicken broth

½ white onion, chopped

1 tablespoon minced fresh ginger

2 stalks lemongrass, chopped

2 fresh limes, juiced

2 tablespoons fish sauce

1 (13½-ounce) can unsweetened
    coconut milk

1 tablespoon Thai red curry paste

Pinch paprika

1 pound udon noodles

2 tablespoons peanut oil

1 pound shrimp, cleaned

2 dozen mussels, steamed

1 cup fresh shiitake mushroom caps

½ cup chopped fresh cilantro

½ cup green onion tendrils

½ cup peanuts, chopped

Serves 4 to 6

Belton Thai Noodle Dish

BELTON CHALET, WEST GLACIER   ✦   CHEF MELISSA MANGOLD

Located just outside Glacier National Park's west entrance, the Swiss-style Belton Chalet was the first of several chalets and lodges to open as part of the Great Northern Railway's effort to lure and accommodate passengers. After more than a century, it still attracts people to the "Crown of the Continent," but they can now feast on one of Chef Mangold's innovative dishes that are as international as the guests who visit.

In a large pot, simmer the chicken broth, onion, ginger, lemongrass, and lime juice together until the liquid is reduced by half. Add the fish sauce, coconut milk, curry paste, and paprika. Cook for 10 minutes.

Cook the udon noodles in salt water until tender, then drain.

Heat the peanut oil in a skillet until very hot, but not smoking, then add the shrimp and cook for about 2 minutes on each side. Add the mussels and shiitake mushrooms and cook until heated through. Strain the sauce over the shellfish and mushrooms.

Add the shellfish and sauce mixture to the noodles and garnish with cilantro, green onion tendrils, and chopped peanuts.

6 (12- to 16-ounce) lamb shanks

Salt and pepper

2 tablespoons canola oil

1½ cups diced yellow onion

1 cup diced carrots

4 garlic cloves, minced

2 teaspoons ground cumin

½ teaspoon ground cinnamon

1 teaspoon ground coriander

½ teaspoon ground ginger

½ teaspoon ground nutmeg

¼ teaspoon ground allspice

½ teaspoon red pepper flakes

1½ cups dry red wine

2 cups low-salt chicken broth

2 cups canned crushed tomatoes
    with juice

2 tablespoons tomato paste

Serves 6

❧ *Chef's Tip: Serve with Timeless Seeds'
Black Beluga Lentils and sautéed
spinach, topped with a dollop of
plain Greek yogurt and a leafy
sprig of cilantro.*

Braised Lamb Shanks with Spices and Tomato

THE PEARL CAFÉ, MISSOULA   ❧   CHEF PEARL CASH

By nature, a braise is never an exact method. This is a taste-and-touch recipe that is ideal when you have a long winter afternoon to commit to dinner. Once the lamb is in the oven, though, you'll have the next three hours free to languish in the savory aroma that will fill the house as a tempting precursor to a deliciously hearty meal.

Begin with all ingredients measured in advance. Salt and pepper the lamb shanks.

In a large heavy pot, heat the canola oil and brown the lamb shanks on all sides. Remove the shanks to a platter, drain off all but a couple of teaspoons of fat, turn the heat to low, and add the onions, carrots, and garlic. Stir, scraping up any brown bits until the onions soften slightly. Add the spices, stirring constantly for a minute until they are fragrant. Do not burn.

Add the wine to the pot and reduce until it just covers the vegetables. Add the broth, crushed tomatoes, and tomato paste. Stir to combine thoroughly. Return the lamb to the pot and bring to a boil.

Braise for 3 hours at 325 degrees. If you are using smaller shanks, test at 2½ hours. The meat should be fork tender and pulling away from the bones.

Remove the lamb from the pot. With a ladle, press the sauce through a coarse sieve or strainer. Some of the cooked vegetables should press through the strainer, especially the tomatoes.

Return the lamb to the pot. At this point the lamb may be cooled, uncovered, and then refrigerated to be finished later. This is preferable, as it allows you to completely degrease the sauce and better blend the flavors.

Degrease the sauce, taste for salt, and bring to a simmer. Add the shanks and turn them to coat with sauce.

½ cup extra virgin olive oil

1 large yellow onion, diced small

3 pounds Yukon potatoes,
    sliced thin

½ cup heavy cream

1 ½ cups grated Parmesan cheese

Salt and pepper

3 pounds ground buffalo (bison)

1 shallot, minced

3 garlic cloves, minced

2 tablespoons dried thyme

2 tablespoons dried basil

1 tablespoon dried oregano

1 cup tomato sauce

Serves 8

Buffalo Hash Parmentier

IZAAK WALTON INN, ESSEX
CORPORATE CHEF EDUARDO LEON

The historic Izaak Walton Inn, bordering Glacier National Park, is a Montana landmark. In addition to the year-round splendor of its location, the famous "dining car" cuisine punctuates a visit to Glacier with savory memories. This hearty dish is much like a shepherd's pie and is the perfect meal following a day of hiking or skiing.

In a medium saucepan, add ¼ cup of olive oil. Heat the oil on medium–high heat, then add the onions and cook until they are translucent. Reduce the burner to medium and add the potatoes, stirring constantly. Once the potatoes begin to soften, add the cream and bring the heat to low. Allow the cream to thicken, cooking for 5 to 10 minutes, and then add ½ cup of Parmesan cheese and season with salt and pepper to taste. Remove from heat and cool.

In another medium saucepan, add the remaining oil over medium heat. Add the ground buffalo and cook until golden brown, stirring to break it into evenly sized pieces. Once the buffalo is cooked, add the shallots, garlic, thyme, basil, and oregano. Mix well, add salt and pepper to taste, and then stir in the tomato sauce; continue to cook for about 10 minutes. Remove from heat.

Prepare a 9 x 13-inch ceramic or metal baking dish with butter or nonstick spray. Line the bottom of the dish with a layer of potatoes, then sprinkle with ½ cup of Parmesan cheese. Using a slotted spoon to avoid adding oil, add all of the cooked buffalo mixture in an even layer. With the spoon, press the buffalo down slightly so it binds better. Add the second half of the potatoes and press them gently to form a relatively flat layer. Sprinkle in the last ½ cup of grated Parmesan cheese and allow the mixture to rest for about 20 minutes.

Cover the dish with aluminum foil and bake in the oven at 375 degrees for 35 minutes. Remove the foil and bake until golden brown, another 10 minutes.

Slice and serve with a fresh garden salad.

Pie dough

1 ½ cups pastry flour

½ teaspoon baking powder

¼ teaspoon salt

⅓ to ½ cup shortening or butter
 or other fat

¼ cup cold water

Filling

½ pound raw beef steak, diced

1 cup chopped onion

1 medium potato, diced

1 cup diced rutabagas (optional)

Salt and pepper

1 tablespoon butter

Serves 2

❧ *Chef's Tip: To keep the pasties from
drying as they bake, check every 15
minutes and drizzle a teaspoon of
hot water into the slits of the pastry.*

Butte Irish Pasties

MRS. MAUREEN HAYES MANSFIELD

This recipe is from the Butte Heritage Cookbook, *produced by the Butte
Silver Bow Arts Foundation. Butte in the 1800s was home to the "copper
kings," whose mining endeavors transformed the open country into "the
richest hill on earth." In its heyday, 100 different nationalities made up the
fabric of Butte, and with them came ethnic food from their home countries.
The pasty (PASS-tee) is one that endured even after the Berkeley Pit was
shut down. It was once the common fare in Cornish and Irish miners'
lunch pails; now there are at least four restaurants that claim their pasty
as Butte's best.*

Preheat the oven to 400 degrees.

To prepare the pie dough:
Sift the flour, baking powder, and salt together. Using your hands,
add the butter or shortening to combine the flour mixture until it
forms pea–sized pieces. Drizzle cold water over the rough dough,
then mix, shape, and roll with a rolling pin. Divide the dough in half.

To prepare the filling:
In a bowl combine the meat, onion, potato, and, if desired, the
rutabaga. Mix well.

To assemble:
Roll one half of the dough to the shape and size of a pie plate, rolled
thin. Pile half the filling on half of the dough to within an inch of
the edge. Sprinkle with salt and pepper, then dot with butter. Fold the
other half of the dough over the filling and press the edges together
well. Repeat with the second piece of dough.

Place the two pasties in the pie plate. Cut three slits in the tops of
each. Bake for 45 minutes at 400 degrees or until well browned, then
reduce the oven to 350 degrees for 15 minutes.

1 cup sliced carrots

1 cup sliced celery

1 cup shallots, cut into rings
    (set aside a few extra
    for the sauce)

⅔ cup sliced wild mushrooms

2 tablespoons butter

Salt and white pepper

3 tablespoons vegetable oil

4 boneless chicken breasts

½ cup Marsala cooking wine

1 cup chicken stock

1 cup heavy cream

2 tablespoons cornstarch slurry
    (optional)

1 teaspoon fresh thyme

Puff pastry, cut into 4 (3-inch) rounds

2 tablespoons butter, melted

Serves 4

Deconstructed Chicken "Pot Pie"

HOLLAND LAKE LODGE, SWAN VALLEY   ✵   CHEF AMBER LUKAS

*Inspired by her Midwestern upbringing, Chef Lukas' twist on this
quintessential comfort food presents beautifully and promises to be
the best-tasting pot pie you've ever had.*

Preheat the oven to 425 degrees.

Lightly sauté the carrots, celery, shallots, and mushrooms in butter
and season with salt and white pepper to taste. Cook thoroughly,
but leave the carrots and celery crisp. Set aside.

Heat the vegetable oil in a large skillet. Rinse the chicken and pat dry,
season with salt and pepper, and sear one side in the hot oil until
brown. Place the chicken in a baking pan, seared side up, and finish
in the 425-degree oven for 7 to 8 minutes.

Use the same skillet to make the sauce. Add a few of the shallots
with butter and sauté until soft. Add the Marsala and ignite with
a long-reach lighter to burn off the alcohol. Be careful! The alcohol
will flame up. When the flames subside, add the chicken stock and
then the cream. (It's fun to flame the sauce, but if you prefer, turn
the burner up to medium-high and allow the alcohol to gradually
cook off.) Simmer and reduce until thickened. If needed, use a roux
or cornstarch slurry to thicken the sauce; about 2 tablespoons of
either should do the trick. Season with salt and pepper to taste
and add the fresh thyme.

Meanwhile, cut four 3-inch rounds from the puff pastry dough.
Brush a heavy metal baking dish with melted butter, set the rounds
in the dish, and lightly brush their tops with butter. Bake in the oven
until they are puffed and golden brown, about 8 to 10 minutes.

Add the vegetables to the sauce and simmer until bubbly. Slice the
chicken. Carefully peel the tops off the puff pastry rounds. Place
the bottom round on a plate, layer with sauce and sliced chicken,
and finish with a pastry top. Serve with extra sauce if desired.

2 racks of Montana lamb,
    frenched

Salt and pepper to taste

Chives

**Fingerling Potatoes
    with Caramelized Onions**
    (see recipe on page 41)

Chimmichurri Sauce
    (see recipe on page 130)

Serves 8

Montana ranks fifth in the country
for lamb production and sixth for
wool production.

Grilled Rack of Lamb
with Chimmichurri Sauce

MOUNTAIN SKY GUEST RANCH, EMIGRANT
CHEF BRIAN BIELEN

*Since it opened in 1929, Mountain Sky has become one of Montana's
most iconic guest ranches. Families return here year after year for the
authentic Western experience and, of course, the excellent meals!*

Prepare a barbecue grill.

Preheat the oven to 350 degrees.

Place the lamb racks on a hot grill and cook 4 to 5 minutes on each
side, then remove from the grill. Place the lamb on a sheet pan and
cook in the oven until an inserted thermometer reads 125 degrees
(for rare) or 135 degrees (for medium rare), 20 to 25 minutes. Remove
the lamb from the oven and let rest for 5 minutes; the lamb will
continue to cook and rise in temperature by 5 to 10 degrees. Slice
the racks into individual chops. Season with salt and pepper to taste.

Presentation:
Place the fingerling potatoes in the center of the plate. Cross three
"frenched" lamb chops over the potatoes, the bones crisscrossing
upright. Tie the bones with a chive stem to hold them together.
Artfully drizzle the lamb and the plate with the chimmichurri sauce.

1 pound ground lamb

1 small onion, diced medium

1 red pepper, diced medium

1 yellow pepper, diced medium

1 teaspoon chopped garlic

1 (8-ounce) can diced tomatoes

1 tablespoon tomato paste

1 teaspoon ground cumin

1 teaspoon ground coriander

1 teaspoon paprika

1 teaspoon Bistro Seasoning Salt
    (see recipe on page 128)

½ teaspoon pepper

24 ounces pappardelle pasta

1 bunch fresh kale or spinach

1 cup Amaltheia Organic Dairy
    goat cheese

Serves 8

Lamb Ragout with Pappardelle

2ND STREET BISTRO, LIVINGSTON
CHEF/PROPRIETOR BRIAN MENGES

"Food is always a story for me," says Brian Menges. *"In a small indie bistro, each dish has its own little story that over time becomes very personal. It is so much more than a recipe."* This dish was created to help local lamb producers, Jim and Barb Marshall of Crazy Woman Farm, create a market not just for their prime cuts (racks and chops), but also for ground meat products. It is a simple meat and tomato sauce driven by cumin and coriander. At the restaurant, they toss with homemade hand-torn pasta, a recipe taught to Chef Menges by Maurizio Albarelo in Barbaresco, Italy. But that is another story.

Slowly simmer the lamb to render the fat. Add the onions, peppers, and garlic and sauté until translucent. Add the canned tomatoes and 1 tablespoon of tomato paste. Add the cumin, coriander, paprika, Bistro Seasoning Salt, and pepper. Simmer for 20 minutes; adjust seasonings to taste.

Cook your choice of pasta—pappardelle if you can find it—or any wide pasta. 2nd Street Bistro serves this dish with homemade hand-torn pasta *(see Chef's Tip)*.

While the pasta cooks, chop the fresh kale or spinach into bite-size pieces. Right before serving, add the chopped fresh greens to the ragout, letting them wilt just slightly; they should still have some leafy form and remain bright green. Plate the pasta and top with the ragout. Garnish with goat cheese.

❧ *Chef's Tip: The Basic Pasta Dough recipe (see recipe on page 127) could be adapted to suit this dish. Make the pasta dough according to the recipe. If using a pasta roller with six width notches, pass the dough through all the settings to the thinnest level. Tear the rolled dough into 2 x 2-inch squares or cut into 2 x 3-inch rectangles. Don't worry about being uniform. Cook the pasta in salted, oiled, and boiling water until al dente. Drain and toss with additional olive oil.*

Crust

1½ to 2 cups macadamia nuts

1 cup panko bread crumbs

½ teaspoon kosher salt

1 teaspoon chopped fresh parsley

1 pinch red pepper flakes

Walleye

6 (6-ounce) fillets fresh walleye

1 cup heavy cream

1 cup peanut oil

Honey-Butter Béchamel Sauce

(see recipe on page 133)

Serves 6

What's the buzz? Montana is one of the top ten states for honey production.

Macadamia-Crusted Fresh Wild Walleye

CONTINENTAL DIVIDE RESTAURANT & BISTRO, ENNIS
CHEF/PROPRIETOR ERIC TRAPP

Unlike local trout, walleye is not as likely to enjoy the practice of catch-and-release thanks to its succulent, flaky flesh. There is no commercial wild harvest available from the United States; the frozen wild product from Canada is acceptable. If possible, use fresh wild walleye fillets, caught on your favorite lake—that's the best. This recipe for walleye has become a Continental Divide favorite.

To prepare the crust:
Using the coarse grating blade on a food processor, grate the macadamia nuts. To avoid making nut butter when you grate, fill the feed tube before turning the machine on, and then press the nuts through quickly.

Pour the grated nuts into a bowl and carefully scrape all nut residue from the processor parts (including any nut butter). Add the panko crumbs to the grated nuts and return to the food processor, now using the normal cutting/mixing blade. Add the salt, parsley, and red pepper flakes. Process in pulses until the mixture is homogeneous. Reserve the crust in a dry, sealed container. The crust will keep for 2 weeks in a cool place.

To prepare the walleye:
Remove the skin from the walleye fillets. Pour a shallow layer of heavy fresh cream into a baking pan large enough to hold a fillet. In a similar pan, pour in an inch–deep layer of the nut crust.

(continued on page 82)

Place a fillet skinned side up in the cream, lift it out and let some of the cream drip off, and then press it into the nut crust cream side down.

With dry fingers, gently place the fillet crust up on a baking sheet. Pat the crust, not too firmly, a few times. Repeat with the remaining fillets and set aside in a cool spot until ready to cook.

Prepare the Honey-Butter Béchamel Sauce (1½ cups) and set aside in a warm spot.

Preheat the oven to 400 degrees.

Place a heavy 12- to 14-inch steel or cast-iron frying pan on medium-high heat, add a light layer of peanut oil (or canola, but not olive), and immediately—and carefully—place a fillet or two in the pan crust side down. (Do not preheat the pan or you will burn the nuts.) Cook 3 to 4 minutes, depending on the thickness of the fillets. When the nuts turn golden brown, it's time to remove the fish. Once the nut-crusted side of the fish is cooked, remove from the pan and place on a parchment-lined baking sheet, uncooked flesh side down. If some of the crust falls off, just scrape it up with the spatula and put it back. Repeat this process until all six fillets are on the baking sheet.

Place the sheet of fillets into the oven and bake until the fish is flaky and fully cooked, 8 to 10 minutes. While the fish is baking, spoon Layered Rice *(see recipe in the Salads & Sides chapter, page 45)* and your choice of vegetables onto serving plates. To serve, carefully lift the walleye fillets and place next to the rice and vegetables; spoon the Honey-Butter Béchamel Sauce on top of the fish.

Maple-Brined Pork Chops with Cranberry Reduction, p. 84

Maple brine

4 cups warm water

2 cups maple syrup

½ cup kosher salt

1 cup sugar

Pork chops

8 (10- to 12-ounce) bone-in
   pork chops

½ gallon maple brine

¼ cup extra virgin olive oil,
   for grilling

Kosher salt and freshly ground
   black pepper

Whipped Yams

(see recipe on page 54)

Cranberry Reduction Sauce

(see recipe on page 131)

8 rosemary sprigs

Serves 8

Maple-Brined Pork Chops with Cranberry Reduction

PARADISE VALLEY GRILL, LIVINGSTON   ❧   CHEF JOSH PASTRAMA

Perfect for an autumn feast, this dish is a balance of sweet and savory. A simple list of ingredients yields a tremendously hearty meal fit for a holiday evening.

To prepare the maple brine:
In a large, lidded container that will hold the ½ gallon of maple brine and the pork chops, plus fit in your refrigerator, add the water, maple syrup, salt, and sugar and mix until dissolved. Add the pork chops, cover tightly, and refrigerate for 12 hours. You can also prepare the Whipped Yams and Cranberry Reduction Sauce ahead of the meal.

To prepare the pork chops:
Fire up the barbecue grill. Remove the chops from the brine onto a clean sheet pan; towel and pat off excess brine. Coat both sides of the chops in olive oil and generously season with salt and pepper. Grill the chops for 5 to 8 minutes on each side (the ideal grill temperature is medium, which means the chop centers will still be pink). Remove from the grill and let rest, covered.

Presentation:
Serve with the whipped yams and blanched broccolini or thinly sliced broccoli. Spoon one cup of yams onto each plate, with your choice of vegetable on the side. Gently lay the chops on top of the yams, ladle with Cranberry Reduction Sauce, and top with rosemary sprigs.

(see photograph on page 83)

2 cups peeled garlic cloves

2 cups vegetable oil

1 side sockeye salmon

¼ cup chopped Kalamata olives

¼ cup crumbled feta cheese

⅛ cup chopped fresh parsley

Serves 8

Mediterranean Salmon

CHICO HOT SPRINGS RESORT, PRAY ❧ CHEF MORGAN MILTON

On a hot summer night, the acidity of the chilled couscous salad and the simple flavors of this flaky fish make for a perfect way to cool off.

For the perfect side to the salmon, prepare the Chilled Couscous Salad *(see recipe in the Salads & Sides chapter, page 40)* a day or two in advance.

Preheat the oven to 350 degrees.

In a 9 x 12-inch cake pan, cover the garlic cloves with the vegetable oil. Cook in the oven until the cloves are brown, 10 to 15 minutes, checking and turning frequently. Pour off two-thirds of the oil and set aside. In a food processor or blender, puree the garlic and the remaining oil into a paste.

In a nonstick pan, heat the leftover roasted garlic oil until the pan is smoking hot. Sear the salmon pieces face down until they caramelize. Remove the salmon from the pan and place face up on a sheet pan. Spread the roasted garlic paste on the salmon pieces.

Bake in the 350-degree oven until the salmon is cooked to medium, for 2 to 5 minutes.

Serve the salmon on a bed of the chilled couscous salad. Garnish with Kalamata olives, crumbled feta, and chopped parsley.

Bacon-tomato compote

1 cup diced bacon

1 shallot, minced

1 garlic clove, minced

1 fresh tomato, diced small

Salt and pepper

Chive-Riesling butter sauce

1 shallot, minced

1 garlic clove, minced

Splash of extra virgin olive oil

½ cup dry Riesling wine

2 tablespoons heavy cream

¼ cup (½ stick) cold butter, diced small

Salt

Nutmeg

2 tablespoons minced fresh chives

Trout

3 fresh, cleaned trout, heads removed

Salt and pepper

2 tablespoons butter, divided

Lemon wedges, for garnish

Montana Rainbow Trout with Braised Cabbage and Sautéed Spaetzle Dumplings

LONE MOUNTAIN RANCH, BIG SKY   ❧   CHEF SCOTTIE BURTON

The historic Lone Mountain Ranch kitchen never disappoints. One part dude ranch, one part fishing lodge, another part cross-country ski retreat, it's all parts authentic Montana. For this recipe the simple flavor and texture of trout gets a touch of structure from complex sauces and comfort-food bulk to be satisfying.

Since trout is quick to cook, prepare the accompanying sides (spaetzle dumplings and braised cabbage) and sauces beforehand.

To prepare the bacon-tomato compote:
In a sauté pan, cook the diced bacon until rendered and golden brown. Add the shallots and garlic and continue cooking for 2 minutes. Add the diced tomato and cook for 1 more minute, seasoning with salt and pepper, then set aside.

To prepare the chive-Riesling butter sauce:
In a saucepan on low heat, gently sweat the shallots and garlic in a little bit of olive oil until they turn translucent and tender, being careful not to burn. Once tender, turn up the flame to medium-high and add the wine, then simmer until reduced by half. Stir in the cream. Turn the flame down to low and add the diced butter, stirring and shaking the pan until the butter has completely melted into the sauce. Adjust the seasoning with a little salt and a scratch of fresh nutmeg. Remove from heat and fold in the chives.

To prepare the trout:
Take three whole trout and cut the fillets by running your knife down each side of the backbone from the inside of the fish (effectively removing the backbone, but leaving the skin on). Place the fillets on a sheet pan flesh side up and season with salt and pepper.

Spaetzle Dumplings
(see recipe on page 52)

Braised Cabbage
(see recipe on page 37)

Serves 6

Montana's trout species include rainbow, brown, brook, lake, bull, redband, and cutthroat trout. Cutthroat, redband, bull, and lake trout are native to Montana's streams and lakes.

With two sauté pans on the stove, melt 1 tablespoon of butter in each. In one pan, add the spaetzle and sauté until golden brown; salt to taste. In the other pan, sauté the trout fillets flesh side down until golden brown, then flip them over to finish. This won't take long, about 3 minutes per side.

Presentation:
Spoon the spaetzle onto the center of a plate and add a tablespoon of the bacon–tomato compote. Place a wedge of the warm braised cabbage on top, then cap with a trout fillet. Spoon the butter sauce over and around the fish and cabbage and garnish with a lemon wedge.

Seasoned flour

3 cups flour

2 tablespoons sea salt

¼ teaspoon pepper

2 tablespoons paprika

½ tablespoon granulated garlic

2 tablespoons onion powder

Pheasant

3 eggs

¼ cup milk

6 boneless, skinless pheasant breasts

¾ cup canola oil

Marsala sauce

2 garlic cloves, minced

1 small yellow onion, julienned

3 cups sliced mushrooms

1 cup Marsala wine

1 cup sweet white wine

2 cups chicken stock

1 lemon, wedged

3 cups fresh spinach,
   coarsely chopped

¼ cup (½ stick) butter

Salt and pepper to taste

Serves 6

Pheasant Marsala

JOHN BOZEMAN'S BISTRO, BOZEMAN
CHEF/PROPRIETOR TYLER HILL

The Bistro is arguably Bozeman's oldest fine-dining establishment. It has endured as a downtown staple for three decades.

To prepare the pheasant:
In a mixing bowl, stir together the flour, salt, pepper, paprika, granulated garlic, and onion powder. Set aside. In a medium bowl, blend the eggs and milk. Dunk the pheasant pieces in the egg mixture, then dredge them one at a time in the seasoned flour blend and pat to coat well. Set aside the pheasant pieces on a plate.

In a large cast-iron skillet or frying pan, heat the canola oil to a very hot temperature (375 degrees). Carefully place the pheasant in the hot oil and cook until golden brown on one side; be careful not to let it burn. Turn the pheasant to brown the other side. Turn back and forth to keep from burning until the pheasant is thoroughly cooked. Check for doneness by cutting into the center of large pieces. The pheasant is done when the meat is white, about 15 minutes in all. Do not overcook! Remove from the skillet and set aside.

To prepare the Marsala sauce:
In the same skillet with the same oil heated back up to temperature, add the garlic and julienned onion. Cook until the onions are nicely caramelized. Add the mushrooms and cook for 3 minutes. Sprinkle in 2 tablespoons of the leftover seasoned flour and stir well. Add the Marsala and white wine and cook for 2 minutes while stirring, then add the chicken stock. Bring to a boil and place the pheasant in the sauce. Simmer for 5 minutes. Squeeze the juice from half a lemon into the sauce and stir in the spinach and butter. Salt and pepper to taste, then remove from heat.

Serve on your favorite pasta or risotto and garnish with the remaining lemon wedges.

1 ½ cups Christian Brothers
    Ruby Port

2 teaspoons chopped fresh thyme

2 teaspoons finely diced shallots

½ cup (1 stick) butter,
    chilled and cubed

Salt and pepper

¼ cup light olive oil for sautéing

8 (6-ounce) red deer loins
    or venison backstraps

Serves 8

Red Deer with Port Wine Butter Sauce

BUCK'S T-4 LODGE, BIG SKY ❧ CHEF CHUCK SCHOMMER

This classic preparation celebrates the rich flavors of the best cut of venison. Buck's T-4 uses red deer imported from New Zealand. If you harvest your own wild game, substitute deer, elk, or pronghorn steaks.

In a saucepan over medium heat, combine the port wine, thyme, and shallots and reduce by a third or until the mixture thickens slightly.

Remove the saucepan from the heat and whisk in the cold butter cubes, constantly stirring the mixture until the butter melts. Season with salt and pepper. Set aside in a warm area until ready to use. (Do not reheat or the sauce will break.)

Season the venison loins with salt and pepper. Preheat a sauté pan over medium heat, add the olive oil, and sauté the venison to your desired doneness.

Serve with Truffle Risotto *(see recipe in the Salads & Sides chapter, page 53)*, freshly grilled asparagus, and the port wine butter sauce.

Potato gnocchi

2 pounds russet potatoes

2 tablespoons kosher salt

3 egg yolks

1 to 4 cups flour

3 tablespoons butter

Mushroom velouté

2 to 3 whole leeks,
   depending on size

¼ cup extra virgin olive oil

Salt and white pepper

1 pound assorted mushrooms:
   crimini, oyster, shiitake,
   porcini, morel, etc.

¼ cup canola oil

4 cups mushroom trimmings
   and button mushrooms

3 tablespoons canola oil

1 large shallot, diced

3 garlic cloves

¼ cup white wine

3 bay leaves

Small bunch fresh thyme

2 quarts cold water

2 teaspoons lemon zest

Russet Potato Gnocchi with Roasted Mushroom Velouté

RAINBOW RANCH LODGE, BIG SKY   ❧   CHEF MATTHEW FRITZ

Don't be intimidated by this long list of ingredients—it's not as hard as it looks, and it is certainly worth the effort for gnocchi that practically melt in your mouth.

To prepare the potato gnocchi:

Rinse the potatoes under cold water and pierce them multiple times with a fork, then lightly dust with kosher salt and bake in a 350-degree oven until tender. While the potatoes are still hot, slice them in half and scoop out the flesh with a spoon. Run it through a food mill or a hand ricer. While still warm, place the riced potatoes into a mixer bowl fitted with a paddle attachment. Add the eggs, kosher salt, and 1 cup of flour and combine on the lowest setting until the mixture is tacky without being sticky; you may or may not need the full amount of flour listed.

Form the potato mixture into "snakes" ½ inch thick; cut those into ¾-inch-long pieces and place them on a floured sheet tray. Once you've formed all the gnocchi, bring a 2-gallon pot of salted water to a boil. Blanch the gnocchi in boiling water until they start to float. Immediately remove them from the water and submerge in an ice bath until cool, about 2 minutes. Remove the gnocchi from the ice bath and set on a kitchen towel to dry, then place dry gnocchi onto a lightly floured sheet pan and reserve for immediate use or freeze.

To prepare the mushroom velouté:

First grill the leeks. Trim away the green upper part of the leeks, leaving about 2 inches of green tops attached to the white bottoms, making sure to leave the root end of the leeks attached. Reserve the trimmed green tops for the velouté.

Split the leeks in half lengthwise and submerge in cold water to remove any dirt imbedded between the layers. Pat dry and season with olive oil, salt, and white pepper. Place the leeks cut side down

Garnish

1 cup grated Parmigiano-Reggiano
   cheese

Truffle oil (optional)

Serves 8

> ✥ *Chef's Tip: If you aren't going to use
> the gnocchi within 24 hours, lightly
> coat them with oil and place them
> in the freezer on a parchment-lined
> baking sheet until frozen. Transfer to
> a sealed container and store for use
> at a later date.*

onto a hot grill and grill for 3 to 4 minutes on each side. Remove and cool, then trim the root off and discard. Cut the grilled leeks into ½-inch pieces and set aside.

Preheat the oven to 350 degrees. To roast the mushrooms, depending on the variety, trim the root end from some (oyster) and stem from others (shiitake). Keep the mushroom trimmings for the sauce. Cut the mushrooms into bite-size pieces, season with salt and white pepper, and drizzle with ¼ cup of canola oil. Place the seasoned mushrooms onto a parchment-lined baking sheet and roast in the oven until the mushrooms start to sweat and brown slightly, about 8 to 10 minutes. Remove from the oven and set aside.

Your mushroom trimmings and other mushroom pieces should total about 4 cups. If you don't have enough trimmings, make up the difference with regular button mushrooms.

Pour 3 tablespoons of canola oil into a 4-quart saucepan and sweat the mushroom trimmings on medium heat until tender. Add the reserved leek tops, shallots, and garlic and cook for an additional 4 minutes, making sure not to burn the garlic. Deglaze the mixture with white wine, add the bay leaves, thyme, and cold water, and bring the mixture to a simmer. Continue to cook, reducing the volume by half.

Once the mixture is reduced, remove and discard the leek tops. Let the mixture cook a few minutes, then puree in a blender until smooth. Pour the mixture back into the saucepan and return to a simmer. Add salt and white pepper to taste and stir in the lemon zest.

Presentation:

If the gnocchi are frozen, remove them from the freezer and bring to room temperature. In a large sauté pan over medium-high heat, melt the butter and sauté the gnocchi until they start to brown. Add the roasted mushroom mixture and grilled leeks and sauté for 3 minutes. Then add the mushroom velouté and heat well. Add salt and white pepper to taste, and garnish with grated Parmigiano-Reggiano cheese and truffle oil if desired. The final dish shouldn't be dry or soupy. Aim for enough velouté in the final product to pool up slightly in the serving dish.

3 pounds skirt steak

4 cloves garlic, rough chopped

¼ cup olive oil

2 tablespoons fresh thyme leaves

1 teaspoon sea salt

1 pound red or green grapes

2 pounds fingerling potatoes

2 cups chicken or duck fat

Salt and pepper

1 cup Rose Hip Jam
   (see recipe on page 138)

Serves 8

Skirt Steak with Rose Hip Jam and Burnt Grapes

J BAR L RANCH, LIMA   ✤   CHEF ANDREW IRVIN-ERICKSON

Skirt steak is one of the most flavorful cuts of meat; it cooks quickly and readily absorbs the flavors of the grill. At the J Bar L Ranch, guests learn about sustainable agriculture through the grass-fed beef program.

To prepare the skirt steak:

First, tenderize the meat by stabbing it repeatedly with a skewer or a small paring knife. You can have a little fun with an ice pick, Sharon Stone style, but don't scare your spouse.

In a plastic bag, combine the garlic, olive oil, thyme, and salt. Place the skirt steak in the bag and massage to coat. Seal the bag and remove as much air as you can, either with a vacuum packer or by slowly submerging the bag in a sink full of cold water until the water comes to the top of the bag. Run your hand up the bag from the meat to the top and then seal. Let stand 2 hours at room temperature or overnight in the refrigerator.

Start the charcoal barbecue with half the amount of charcoal you would usually use. Add that same amount of raw hickory or your favorite hardwood (the larger the pieces the better). Grill the skirt steak over the highest heat possible, constantly moving and flipping it to allow each side to rest in between blasts of intense heat. Remove from the grill and let the meat rest for 5 to 10 minutes on a cutting board.

To prepare the burnt grapes:

Remove the grill from the barbecue and place the bunches of grapes right onto the burning hardwood and charcoal embers. Allow the grapes to spit and char before flipping. Remove from the embers and let rest for 5 minutes. Don't serve hot grapes—the juice will squirt and burn! Pull the stems before serving.

To prepare the potatoes:

In a large pot, simmer the potatoes until they just begin to soften, then drain. With a heavy knife, gently press the potatoes until they collapse, without smashing them flat. Fry them in duck fat until crisp, then flip and crisp the other side. Liberally season with salt and pepper.

Presentation:

Slice the skirt steak against the grain into ¼–inch strips and arrange on a plate. Spoon Rose Hip Jam on the side next to the meat, top with burnt grapes, and serve with potatoes and grilled vegetables of your choice.

HOME ON THE RANGE: J BAR L RANCH

With a holistic management approach that prevents overgrazing, fosters wildlife diversity, and leaves a minimal carbon footprint, the 9,000-acre J Bar L Ranch is the largest producer of Montana-raised beef. That's a surprising fact, considering that there are 2.5 million beef cattle in the state from hundreds of ranches, while the J Bar L Ranch brings just 300 cows to market each year. The defining factor is that the J Bar L Ranch's beef is raised in Montana, slaughtered in Billings, and sold either direct to the buyer or to restaurants throughout the region; other ranches sell to a regional corporate slaughterhouse, which buys cows "on the hoof" from stockyards, slaughters en masse, and distributes the beef throughout the country with no definite origin.

For a taste of Montana-raised beef, look for Yellowstone Grass-fed Beef on local menus throughout the state.

Tagliatelle

24 ounces tagliatelle pasta

4 cups wild mushroom mix

2 tablespoons vegetable oil

Pinch salt

2 teaspoons minced shallots

2 teaspoons minced garlic

4 cups pulled chicken
(from 1 whole roasted chicken)

4 cups Tag Sauce
(see recipe on page 140)

Salt and pepper

Garnish

Freshly shaved Parmesan cheese

Chives, chopped

Drizzle of white truffle oil
(optional but strongly suggested)

Serves 8

Tagliatelle with Wild Mushrooms

LATITUDE 48°, WHITEFISH   CHEF JAMES TRAVIS MANNING

Simple and savory, this mushroom sauce coats the ribbons of pasta for a satisfying vegetarian option.

Bring a large pot of water to a boil and lightly season with salt. Once the water is at a rolling boil, add the pasta. When the pasta is al dente, drain and set aside. Sauté the mushrooms in 2 tablespoons of hot oil with a heavy pinch of salt. When the mushrooms are tender, add the shallots and garlic and cook for 1 more minute, tossing constantly to keep from burning. Then add the chicken and Tag Sauce. Season to taste with salt and freshly ground pepper. Add the cooked pasta to the sauce, chicken, and mushroom mixture. Cook the noodles for another 2 to 3 minutes in the sauce before plating each serving.

Garnish with Parmesan cheese, chives, and truffle oil.

Foragers revel in finding fungi in Montana. Some of the more common, yet often elusive, crops are bolete, chanterelles, oysters, puffballs, and morels. Proper identification is essential—many poisonous species closely resemble edible mushrooms.

1 1/2 cups milk

1/2 cup (1 stick) butter

1 pound pure Italian-grade
    durham wheat elbow macaroni

1 pound Velveeta® cheese

1 1/2 cups grated smoked
    Gouda cheese

1 1/4 teaspoons coarsely ground
    black pepper

2 cups grated low-moisture,
    part-skim mozzarella cheese

Serves 8 to 10

Wild West Mac and Cheese

WILD WEST PIZZERIA, WEST YELLOWSTONE
CHEF/PROPRIETOR AARON HECHT

Undeniably, Wild West Pizzeria has excellent pizza, but the best-kept secret is the Mac and Cheese. After a winter day in Yellowstone National Park or on the cross-country ski trails near West, there is nothing better than a molten 12-ounce portion of this full-fat, three-cheese, oven-finished treat.

Combine the milk and butter in a large saucepan and heat until the butter has melted into the milk. At the same time, bring a pot of water to a boil and cook the macaroni noodles al dente.

Cut the Velveeta® into 2–inch cubes and add to the butter and milk mixture. Add the smoked Gouda and black pepper. Cook until the sauce is completely melted and smooth.

Preheat the oven to 450 degrees. When the macaroni has finished cooking, drain and rinse in cold water. Combine the macaroni noodles and sauce and place in a greased casserole dish. Cover the entire top of the noodle mixture with the mozzarella cheese and bake, uncovered, until the cheese is golden brown and bubbling, about 25 minutes.

❧ *Chef's Tip: Add your favorite uncooked ground meats and vegetables to make this a dinner entrée. For the best "meltable" cheese, it's all about the Velveeta®!*

According to aficionados, Yellowstone caviar rivals the exclusive Russian Seruga caviar. The caviar is harvested from native Montana paddlefish each year from May 15 through June near Glendive. The delicate black roe retails for $40 per ounce.

Desserts & Sweet Treats

Coconut Cream Pie, p. 102

1 pound (16 large) Medjool dates

1 cup (8 ounces) almond paste

½ cup (1 stick) butter, melted

½ cup light olive oil

1 pound phyllo dough

3 tablespoons ground cinnamon

¼ cup powdered sugar

Serves 16

Almond-Filled Dates in Phyllo

KAFÉ UTZA, MILES CITY   ❧   CHEF KARA BROWNING

This dish is inspired by a love of Mediterranean regional ingredients. Designed with intense flavor and texture, the simplicity is unforgettable!

Slice the dates and remove the pits. Cut the almond paste into sixteen equal portions. Shape each portion into an oval and insert into a sliced date. Set the stuffed dates aside.

In a small bowl, blend the melted butter with the olive oil. Set a soft-bristle pastry brush next to the bowl. Working quickly, unfold one package of dough (about twenty sheets) with the long side facing you. Slice the phyllo in half from top to bottom. Wrap one half in plastic to prevent it from drying out. Working with the remaining stack, layer and brush five phyllo leaves with the butter and oil mixture, starting at the edges and moving to the center. Sprinkle a liberal amount of cinnamon in a 1-inch-wide path down the center, from top to bottom. Place a filled date on the lower edge of the cinnamon path and roll it up in the dough. Gently pinch the dough closed to resemble a cellophane-wrapped candy. Repeat this process, using five leaves per date.

Arrange the phyllo-wrapped dates 1 inch apart on a baking sheet lightly oiled with cooking spray. (If preparing in advance, you can cover and freeze the whole sheet for up to 2 weeks. Thaw before baking.)

Preheat the oven to 350 degrees; bake the phyllo-wrapped dates for 15 minutes. Remove from oven, cool briefly, and dust the top of each confection with powdered sugar.

❧ *Chef's Tip: Check the expiration date before buying phyllo dough; fresh phyllo will be pliable and tender and much easier to work with. Frozen phyllo can be thawed in the refrigerator and kept there for up to 30 days, or thawed at room temperature for at least 2 hours. Almond paste can usually be found with pie fillings in the baking aisle of your local market. Also look for Vietnamese cinnamon; it is higher in essential oils.*

2 cups flour

2 cups sugar

2 teaspoons baking soda

2 teaspoons ground cinnamon

1 teaspoon salt

1 ½ cups vegetable oil

4 eggs

3 cups shredded carrots

Cream Cheese Frosting
(see recipe on page 132)

Serves 12

Carrot Cake with Cream Cheese Frosting

HANGIN' ART GALLERY, ARLEE   ❧   CHEF DONNA MOLLICA

What looks like a roadside coffee shop in the strip of the Jocko Valley is actually an essential community hall, gallery, bakery, and gathering place. Friends return again and again to share a slice of this timeless cake.

Preheat the oven to 350 degrees. Grease and flour 2 (8-inch) round cake pans.

In a large bowl, sift together the flour, sugar, baking soda, cinnamon, and salt. Stir in the vegetable oil and mix until just blended. Add the eggs and stir until blended. Fold in the shredded carrots; the batter will be fairly stiff. Divide evenly between the two pans and gently shake the pans to spread out the batter.

Bake until a toothpick inserted into the cake comes out clean, 40 to 45 minutes. Cool in the pans on a wire rack for 10 minutes. Use a spatula to gently separate the cake from the sides of the pans, and then tip the cakes from the pans onto wire racks to cool completely.

Frost with Cream Cheese Frosting.

4 cups milk

¼ cup sugar

1 teaspoon ancho chili powder

Pinch sea salt

½ cup (4 ounces) dark chocolate (70% cocoa solids), chopped

½ cup (4 ounces) bittersweet chocolate (60% cocoa solids), chopped

Serves 8

Chocolat Chaud (Hot Chocolate)

LA CHATELAINE CHOCOLAT CO., BOZEMAN
CHOCOLATIERS WLADY GROCHOWSKI
AND SHANNON HUGHES GROCHOWSKI

Walk into La Chatelaine Chocolat Co. and the aroma of exotic chocolates is intoxicating. The truffles are unparalleled in Montana, but while waiting for a box of handmade chocolates, don't miss the chance to try this bubbly Chocolat Chaud.

In a saucepan, bring the milk and sugar to a boil. Remove from heat and stir in the ancho chili powder and sea salt. Add the chopped chocolates and let stand for 1 minute. Whisk the melted chocolate and milk mixture until frothy. Serve immediately.

❧ *Chef's Tip: Try adding special flavors, such as espresso or rum. Top with whipped cream or crème fraîche. This can also be refrigerated and served cold, over ice cubes, or blended with shaved ice. Voilà!*

½ cup (1 stick) butter

¾ cup (6 ounces) semi-sweet
chocolate chips

¼ cup unsweetened cocoa powder

¾ cup sugar

½ cup heavy cream

1 tablespoon corn syrup

Makes 2 cups

Chocolate Sauce

HOLLAND LAKE LODGE, SWAN VALLEY   ❧   CHEF NANCY WOHLFEIL

*This is one of those kitchen cupboard must-haves. Once you make it
you will realize how versatile this sauce can be. Think hot fudge sundaes,
parfaits, layering for Stuck in a Rut Mud Pie (see recipe on page 124),
or as a drizzle on Red Velvet Cupcakes (see recipe on page 119).*

Combine all the ingredients in a heavy saucepan and simmer, stirring
continuously. Bring to a slow boil for 2 minutes and remove from
heat. Serve warm over gourmet ice cream or your choice of desserts.
Store in an airtight container and refrigerate; the chocolate sauce
will keep for up to a month. It can be reheated in a microwave.

FROM MOO TO YOU: KALISPELL KREAMERY

*At the Hedstrom Dairy, the cows are part of the family. Walking around the
barnyard on the farm her family has worked for thirty-five years, Mary Tuck
recalls how her parents, Bill and Marilyn Hedstrom, started with just one milk
cow. The relationship with that one cow eventually grew into a full-fledged dairy
and a family lifestyle in Flathead County.*

*Today, two generations of farmers work together (with a third growing into
those farmers boots, too) to offer Montana milk that is produced, processed, and
bottled on-site at Kalispell Kreamery. Mary's parents still run the dairy operation, while she and her husband, Jared, handle the creamery. With 150 Holstein
cows producing up to 1,200 pounds (about 140 gallons) of milk per day on
the twenty-five-acre farm, that adds up to a lot of milk and cookies. Kalispell
Kreamery minimally processes its milk, so there are no growth hormones added,
and the raw milk is pasteurized (to kill bacteria) but not homogenized, so cream
forms on top. It is available in grocery stores throughout Montana.*

¾ cup (6 ounces) cream of coconut (Coco López® brand)

¼ cup milk

1 ¼ cups (10 ounces) mini marshmallows

3 cups heavy cream

2 teaspoons coconut extract

2 cups shredded coconut

Your favorite pie shell, baked (see recipes on page 129 or page 131)

Serves 8

Coconut Cream Pie

POMPEY'S GRILL, SACAJAWEA HOTEL, THREE FORKS
CHEF MATTHEW ISRAEL

In a twist on this country classic, Chef Israel suggests getting creative with the pie crust in this recipe. Try a "deconstructed" approach, with the coconut cream filling at the bottom of a plate and a prebaked crust artfully laid on top. Or use cookies instead, by layering them in a parfait cup and topping with more cookies. This is one of those rare moments when a chef says, "It's up to you."

In a double boiler, mix the cream of coconut with the milk, then add the marshmallows and melt. Remove from heat and allow to cool. Once the mixture is cooled, pour it into a 5-quart stand mixer and whip until the volume has increased by at least a third. Transfer the mixture to a large mixing bowl. Pour the heavy cream and coconut extract into the stand mixer and whip until firm peaks form. Gently fold this into the marshmallow mixture. Gently fold in 1 cup of the shredded coconut, making sure it does not clump.

Toast the other cup of shredded coconut for garnish. Preheat the oven to 350 degrees. Spread the shredded coconut on a baking sheet and roast for 8 to 10 minutes, watching closely to prevent burning.

Pour the pie filling into the desired pie shell, parfait glass, or whatever is on your creative mind. Refrigerate for at least 6 hours. Garnish with toasted coconut and sliced strawberries.

❧ **Chef's Tip:** *For the chef's presentation pictured on page 97, use the Coconut Cream Pie Crust recipe on page 131. For a more traditional pie crust, see the Butter Crust Pie Dough on page 129.*

(see photograph on page 97)

Cake

1 ⅔ cup flour

¾ cup unsweetened cocoa powder

1 ½ teaspoons baking powder

½ teaspoon salt

1 ¼ cups (2½ sticks) butter, softened

1 ½ cups brown sugar,
  firmly packed

3 eggs, room temperature

⅓ cup dark molasses

1 ½ cups Guinness stout,
  room temperature

Glossy chocolate icing

½ cup (1 stick) butter

1 ½ cups sugar

1 ½ cups unsweetened
  cocoa powder

1 ¼ cups heavy whipping cream

¼ cup sour cream

1 tablespoon instant coffee granules

2 teaspoons vanilla extract

Serves 8

Dark Chocolate Stout Cake

THE GRAND HOTEL, BIG TIMBER & CHEF AMY SMITH

*Tying the history of comfort food in the elegant bed and breakfast
of The Grand with the rugged edge of the saloon, this rich, chocolaty
Bundt cake gets its richness from the beer.*

To prepare the cake:
Preheat the oven to 350 degrees.

In a large bowl, sift together the flour, cocoa, baking powder, and
salt. Set aside. With a stand mixer, cream together the butter and
brown sugar until fluffy. Add one egg at a time, stopping to scrape
the bowl. Add the molasses; the batter will be lumpy. Slowly add
the flour mixture, alternating with the stout. Beat until smooth,
about 1 minute.

Spoon the batter into a lightly greased Bundt pan or 8-inch round
pan. Bake until a toothpick inserted into the cake comes out clean,
40 to 50 minutes.

To prepare the icing:
Melt the butter in a large saucepan over medium heat. Stir in the
sugar and cocoa, forming a thick, grainy paste. In a separate bowl,
combine the heavy whipping cream, sour cream, and instant coffee
granules and mix until smooth. Gradually add this to the chocolate
mixture and blend until smooth. Cook until the sugar is dissolved
and the icing is smooth and hot; do not boil. Stir in the vanilla
extract and cool to room temperature.

Drizzle icing over the cooled cake and serve.

Cake

¾ cup (1 ½ sticks) plus
    2 tablespoons butter

1 cup (8 ounces) semi-sweet
    chocolate, chopped

¼ cup (2 ounces) unsweetened
    chocolate, chopped

1 cup sugar

5 eggs, separated

¼ cup ground almonds

Glaze

½ cup heavy cream

3 tablespoons butter

½ cup (4 ounces) semi-sweet
    chocolate, chopped

½ cup (4 ounces) milk chocolate,
    chopped

Garnish

Fresh raspberries

Mint leaves

Serves 10

Flourless Chocolate Cake

BUCK'S T-4 LODGE, BIG SKY   ❧   CHEF CHUCK SCHOMMER

Death by chocolate in the Wild West.

To prepare the cake:
Preheat the oven to 350 degrees. Grease an 8- or 10-inch cake pan with shortening.

In a saucepan, melt the butter and semi-sweet and unsweetened chocolates, stirring until smooth. Pour into a large bowl and allow to cool slightly. Add the sugar, egg yolks, and ground almonds and whisk until smooth. Using a mixer and a separate bowl, beat the egg whites until stiff peaks form. Gently fold the whites into the batter half at a time.

Pour the batter into the prepared cake pan and bake until the top begins to crack and a toothpick inserted into the cake comes out clean, about 40 minutes.

Transfer the cake to a wire rack and allow to cool for 15 minutes. Press down gently on the top of the cake to even the edges. Cool completely.

To prepare the glaze:
In a medium saucepan, bring the cream and butter to a simmer. Reduce heat, add the chopped chocolates, and stir until smooth. Let stand about 1 hour.

Invert the cake onto a cardboard round and place on a rack over a baking sheet. Pour the glaze over the cake, spreading to coat the top and sides. Refrigerate. Let the cake stand at room temperature 2 hours before serving.

Garnish with fresh raspberries and mint leaves.

Lemon Chiffon Cake

(see recipe on page 135)

1 loaf wide-cut sourdough
    or French bread

6 whole eggs

3 egg yolks

2 cups heavy cream

1 cup milk

¾ cup sugar

Pinch kosher salt

1 teaspoon vanilla extract

2½ to 3 cups fresh
    or frozen huckleberries

Huckleberry Crème Anglaise
    (optional) *(see recipe
    on page 134)*

Serves 10 to 12

Huckleberry-Lemon Bread Pudding

TWO SISTERS CAFÉ, BABB   ♫   CHEF SUSAN HIGGINS

Essentially this is a dessert within a dessert, if you count the Lemon Chiffon Cake, but the effort is well worth the return in decadence.

Cut the Lemon Chiffon Cake into 1-inch cubes. Spread them on a sheet pan and let them dry while you work on the rest of the recipe.

Preheat the oven to 350 degrees.

Cut the bread into 1-inch cubes. If you are using loaf bread, you may cut off the crusts; if using French bread, do not trim. Spread the bread cubes on a baking sheet and toast in the oven to a golden brown, about 15 minutes; let cool.

To make the custard, in a large bowl whisk together the eggs and egg yolks with the cream, milk, sugar, salt, and vanilla extract until fully combined with no trace of egg white still showing.

After the toasted bread cubes have cooled, toss them with the cake cubes in a large mixing bowl, then pour the custard mixture over the cubes and toss until all the cubes are coated. The cake will probably dissolve down to crumbs; try to keep the cake cubes as intact as possible, but don't worry if they turn to crumbs.

In a large rectangular baking dish, evenly layer about half of the bread pudding mixture. Sprinkle the huckleberries evenly over the first layer of bread pudding (if using frozen huckleberries, first thaw completely and drain well). Spread as evenly as possible, but not so thick that the huckleberries conceal the bread pudding completely (this will allow the layers to stick together). Wash your hands and then layer the rest of the bread pudding over the berries. To prevent mixing the berries and the bread pudding, gently drop medium handfuls of the pudding over the berries and carefully spread out.

Cover with aluminum foil and bake for about 45 minutes in a 350-degree oven. The mixture should be slightly loose, but not liquid, in the center. Remove the aluminum foil and put the baking dish back into the 350-degree oven to brown for about 20 minutes. Keep an eye on it to prevent burning!

Remove from the oven and allow to set up for about 20 minutes. To serve, scoop the bread pudding warm from the pan, top with a generous amount of Huckleberry Crème Anglaise, and, for true decadence, a dollop of whipped cream.

FRESH FARM: GALLATIN VALLEY BOTANICAL

The crop list at Gallatin Valley Botanical is pretty simple: tomatoes, greens, beans, peas, onions, herbs, squash, potatoes, and carrots. But a closer look reveals over 150 varieties of these basic veggies—three different kinds of cabbage, nine types of onions, eleven summer and winter squashes, six different tomatoes, four melon varietals, and over a dozen salad greens, plus more exotic offerings that include Jerusalem artichokes, celeriac, kohlrabi, edible flowers, and eggplant, to name a few.

Simple, yet diverse, and sustainable is the motto for farmers Matt and Jacky Rothschiller, whose small farm near Bozeman supplies 150 Community Supported Agriculture (CSA) shares, a dozen restaurants, the Bozeman Community Food Co-op, and regular farmers' markets in the Gallatin Valley. On just six acres they grow 150 different varieties of vegetables, all natural, pesticide free, and healthy.

½ cup (1 stick) butter, softened

1 ¼ cups sugar, divided

2 eggs

2 cups flour

1 teaspoon baking soda

½ teaspoon salt

1 cup sour cream

1 teaspoon ground cinnamon

1 teaspoon vanilla extract

½ cup fresh huckleberries

½ cup chopped walnuts

Serves 6 to 8

Huckleberry-Sour Cream Coffee Cake

GOOD MEDICINE LODGE, WHITEFISH   CHEF BETSY COX

At the Good Medicine Lodge table, breakfast is the best meal of the day thanks to the talents of Chef Cox, author of the Good Montana Morning *cookbook. Known as one of the loveliest bed and breakfasts in the state, the lodge is an ideal destination not only for its proximity to Glacier Park and the town of Whitefish, but also lakeshore fun, kayaking, fishing, hiking, biking, and skiing. If that doesn't convince you, the good food will.*

Preheat the oven to 350 degrees. Use butter to grease a 10-inch tube pan or 8-inch round pan and dust with flour to prevent the cake from sticking.

In a large bowl, cream the butter with 1 cup of sugar. Add the eggs and blend well. In another bowl, sift the flour, baking soda, and salt together and gradually add it, alternating with the sour cream, to the egg mixture. Pour half of the batter into the pan and spread evenly.

Combine the remaining ¼ cup of sugar, cinnamon, and vanilla extract. Spread half of this onto the batter in the pan. Sprinkle with ¼ cup of huckleberries and ¼ cup of walnuts. Spread the remaining batter and sprinkle with the remaining cinnamon mixture, berries, and nuts.

Bake for 50 to 60 minutes.

  Chef's Tip: If huckleberries are scarce, you may substitute blueberries. If you use frozen berries, do not thaw; add them quickly and place the cake in the oven before they begin to soften and drain. This will retain the juice in the berries and keep the pastry from becoming mushy.

Huckleweizen Beer Ice Cream, p. 110

6 (12-ounce) bottles Yellowstone
    Valley Brewing Co.'s
    Huckleweizen beer

1 ½ tablespoons fresh
    Drange Apiaries honey

1 cup huckleberries

16 egg yolks

3 cups Lifeline Dairy heavy cream

1 cup Crème Fraîche
    (see recipe on page 132)

1 ½ cups sugar in the raw

2 teaspoons kosher or sea salt

Makes ½ gallon

Huckleweizen Beer Ice Cream

CAFÉ DECAMP, BILLINGS   ❧   CHEF/PROPRIETOR JASON DECAMP

Fiercely dedicated to creating a menu around Montana ingredients and local products, Chef DeCamp concocted this unique sabayon-based ice cream. The element of a local microbrew adds an intense flavor that renders the treat almost savory. To complement the yeasty undertones, serve with a sweet, crunchy cookie.

In a large stockpot, reduce the Huckleweizen beer to a scant 2 cups. While the beer reduces, in a separate bowl combine the honey and huckleberries, stirring gently to avoid squishing the berries. Separate the egg yolks into a large mixing bowl and hold at room temperature.

When the beer is reduced, add the heavy cream, Crème Fraîche, sugar, and salt to the reduction and bring it to a very gentle boil, stirring continuously. Allow this soft simmer to carry on for 4 to 5 minutes.

Temper the egg yolks to make a sabayon base by ladling a little of the hot cream into the eggs using a ½-cup ladle or measuring cup. Whisk steadily throughout this step. Whisk about 1½ cups of cream into the yolks, ½ cup at a time, and then add the rest of the cream base, returning it to the flame in the same pot used for the cream. Again, bring to a light simmer, whisking constantly. You can allow for some very small, slow-bursting bubbles to form near the walls of the pot, but nothing more than that. Be sure to stir continuously and visually check to make sure you aren't curdling your eggs. Once the sabayon has thickened enough to thoroughly coat a wooden spoon's backside, remove from the heat; add the honey and huckleberries. Cool completely and refrigerate for 6 hours or overnight.

Churn in an electric ice cream maker according to the machine's instructions until a nice, thick consistency is reached, then freeze. Serve with a cookie of your choice.

(see photograph on page 109)

Cookies

1 ½ cups (3 sticks) butter

1 cup sugar

1 teaspoon vanilla extract

3 ½ cups flour

¼ teaspoon salt

1 tablespoon dried lavender

Glaze

1 cup powdered sugar

2 tablespoons water

1 teaspoon dried lavender

Makes 1 dozen

Lavender Shortbread Cookies

PARK AVENUE BAKERY, HELENA   CHEF KATHERINE BALLEIN

The balance of lavender with the buttery shortbread is a subtle flavor in this recipe and makes a wonderful complement to tea.

Preheat the oven to 350 degrees.

To prepare the cookies:
In a large mixing bowl, cream the butter and sugar until pale but not fluffy; add the vanilla extract and mix until incorporated. Add the flour, salt, and lavender; mix until the dough comes together. Refrigerate until the dough is firm.

Roll the dough out ¼ inch thick and cut with a cookie cutter. Bake until the cookies are firm in the center but not browned, 12 to 14 minutes.

To prepare the glaze:
Whisk the powdered sugar, water, and lavender together until the sugar is dissolved. Dip the top of each cookie into the glaze and let the excess run off. Place the cookies on wax paper and allow to dry overnight.

Lemon curd tart

1 (9-inch) tart crust, prebaked
   (see recipe on page 141)

5 whole eggs

5 egg yolks

1 ½ cups sugar

1 cup fresh lemon juice

½ cup (1 stick) butter, cut in pieces

Huckleberry sauce

3 cups fresh or frozen huckleberries

¼ cup sugar

¼ cup water

2 tablespoons crème de cassis

1 ½ tablespoons cornstarch

Garnish

2 cups whipped cream

8 Johnny-jump-up blossoms

8 mint sprigs

Serves 8

Lemon Curd Tart with Huckleberry Sauce

THE PEARL CAFÉ, MISSOULA   ❧   CHEF PEARL CASH

This long-standing Missoula restaurant serves country cuisine that is out of the ordinary and filled with thoughtful nuance. Chef Cash dubbed this recipe her "foolproof" lemon curd, and the effort produces the most lovely of desserts.

To prepare the lemon curd:
In a heavy-bottomed saucepan, thoroughly stir together the whole eggs, five additional yolks, sugar, lemon juice, and butter. Place over medium heat and whisk until the sauce thickens and the butter is melted. Immediately strain into the prebaked and cooled tart crust. Refrigerate for at least 2 hours.

To prepare the huckleberry sauce:
In a large saucepan over medium heat, stir together 2 cups of huckleberries and the sugar. (If you're using frozen berries, first thaw the berries and drain well.) In a separate bowl, mix the water, crème de cassis, and cornstarch. (If you're using frozen berries, add an extra teaspoon of cornstarch.) Add this mixture to the berries and sugar and cook until thickened and shiny.

Remove from heat and cool for 10 minutes, stirring once or twice. Stir in the remaining cup of berries. Cool at room temperature.

Presentation:
To serve, cut the tart into eight pieces. Place on serving plates and pour the huckleberry sauce over the top quarter of the tart and around the edge. Garnish with a swirl of whipped cream, a Johnny-jump-up blossom, and a mint sprig.

Cupcakes

5 eggs, separated,
    room temperature

2 cups sugar

½ cup (1 stick) butter,
    room temperature

½ cup shortening

1 teaspoon vanilla extract

1 teaspoon baking soda

1 cup buttermilk, room temperature

1 teaspoon salt

2 cups sifted flour

Candied bacon

6 slices thick, high-quality bacon,
    not too lean

¼ cup brown sugar

Maple buttercream

1 ½ cups (3 sticks) butter,
    room temperature

¾ cup shortening,
    room temperature

1 cup (8 ounces) cream cheese,
    room temperature

¼ cup cornstarch

8 cups powdered sugar

2 teaspoons vanilla extract

¼ cup maple syrup

Maple-Bacon Cupcakes

HARPER & MADISON BAKERY AND CAFÉ, BILLINGS
CHEF JOANNIE SWORDS

That's right, bacon on the cupcakes. It sounds bizarre, but the combination of maple buttercream and candied bacon resembles that culinary comfort of bacon dipped in maple syrup with your pancakes, and the chipotle cream filling deepens the decadence, while somehow offsetting the sweetness.

To prepare the cupcakes:
Preheat the oven to 325 degrees.

Use an electric mixer on high speed to beat the egg whites until soft peaks form. Gradually add ½ cup of sugar and continue beating to a meringue-like consistency. Set aside.

In a separate bowl, cream the butter, shortening, remaining 1½ cups of sugar, and vanilla extract. Add the egg yolks one at a time until well blended.

In a separate bowl, stir the baking soda into the buttermilk. Set aside.

Sift the salt together with the flour and then add to the butter mixture, alternating with the buttermilk, beginning and ending with the flour. Gently fold the egg whites into the batter until blended.

Line a muffin tin with paper cups and fill each about two-thirds full with batter. Bake until a toothpick inserted into the center of a cupcake comes out clean, 20 to 25 minutes.

To prepare the candied bacon:
Place the bacon slices on parchment paper on a baking sheet. Sprinkle 2 teaspoons of brown sugar evenly onto each bacon slice. Bake at 300 degrees until well done, about 15 minutes. Remove the bacon immediately from the parchment to prevent it from sticking. Allow to cool.

Chipotle filling

¾ cup (6 ounces) cream cheese, softened

2 tablespoons sugar

1 teaspoon adobo (sauce from canned chipotle peppers)

½ cup heavy whipping cream

Makes 12 large cupcakes

Carnivores eat meat. Herbivores eat plants. Locavores eat food grown within 300 miles of home. Food that is locally grown tastes better because it's fresher (usually picked within twenty-four hours of coming to market) and it's healthier (fruits and vegetables eaten at the height of ripeness have the highest level of nutrients).

To prepare the maple buttercream:
In a mixing bowl, blend together the butter, shortening, and cream cheese. In a separate bowl, sift together the cornstarch and powdered sugar. Add this to the butter mixture and mix until incorporated. Add the vanilla extract and mix until well blended, then thoroughly blend in the maple syrup.

To prepare the chipotle filling:
Mix the cream cheese with the sugar until well blended. Drain the adobo from a small can of chipotle peppers and add the sauce and the heavy cream to the cream cheese mixture. Blend well.

To assemble:
Hollow out the center of a cupcake with a spoon. Fill the hole with chipotle filling. Then top the cupcake with a generous slather of maple buttercream. Place a half slice of candied bacon on top. Repeat these steps to complete all the cupcakes.

3 cups heavy cream

¾ cup milk

⅓ cup sugar

1 teaspoon vanilla extract

3 tablespoons Grand Marnier

9 egg yolks

Sugar for caramelizing

Rind of one orange

Serves 6

Orange Crème Brûlée

FIREHOLE RANCH, WEST YELLOWSTONE
CHEFS BRUNO AND KRIS GEORGETON

This historic lodge, named after the dramatic Firehole River, offers fly fishing enthusiasts an unforgettable retreat. Nestled on the shores of Hebgen Lake, the 1940s-era main lodge and cabins have been lovingly maintained to retain their original style, elegance, and grace. Chefs Bruno and Kris, a husband and wife team, bring luxurious French influences to this rustic getaway.

In a large saucepan, combine the cream, milk, sugar, vanilla extract, and Grand Marnier. Stir gently to help dissolve the sugar. Heat just to a simmer and let steep for 5 to 10 minutes.

In a separate mixing bowl, whisk the egg yolks together. Temper the yolks with the hot cream mixture, by slowly adding the cream and stirring constantly to prevent the egg yolks from cooking. Very lightly whisk the mixture, then strain and skim off any excess foam. Gently pour into eight 6-ounce ramekins.

Set the ramekins in a water bath and bake at 325 degrees until set, about 50 to 60 minutes. Remove the ramekins and refrigerate until well chilled.

Sprinkle with sugar and use a propane torch to caramelize. Garnish with wide strips of orange rind cut with a vegetable peeler. Serve immediately.

Montana tribes have long used chokecherries in making pemmican and for medicinal purposes. The fruit is also favored for jellies, syrups, sauces, jams, and wine. Lewistown hosts a Chokecherry Festival every August.

Tart shell

¾ cup flour

Pinch salt

½ cup (1 stick) butter, cubed and thoroughly chilled

6 tablespoons cold water

Filling

2 pounds pears, cored, peeled, and sliced

2 tablespoons butter

1 ½ tablespoons finely chopped fresh ginger

2 tablespoons raw sugar

Pinch nutmeg

½ cup (4 ounces) white chocolate, shaved

Sabayon

2 egg yolks

2 tablespoons sugar

1 teaspoon ground cardamom

¼ cup cava

¼ cup heavy cream

Serves 8

Pear-Ginger and White Chocolate Tart with Cardamom Sabayon

CAFÉ KANDAHAR, WHITEFISH ❧ CHEF ANDY BLANTON

The key to this elegant tart is to handle the pears gently after cooking. It's a recipe that works with any variety of pear, even Bartletts, which are known to fall apart when cooked, but this light-touch approach defies that rule. Look for local fruit in the fall.

To prepare the tart shell:
In a large bowl, combine the flour and salt. Work the butter into the flour by rubbing chunks of butter between your fingers until pea-size chunks form. Add the water and gently mix into the dough until just combined. Do not knead or overwork the dough. Allow it to rest for at least 1 hour or overnight in the refrigerator.

Roll the chilled dough out and line a 9-inch or bigger tart pan buttered and dusted with flour to keep the crust from sticking.

To prepare the filling:
Preheat the oven to 375 degrees. In a large skillet, warm the pears, butter, and ginger over medium-high heat. Cook until the pears begin to soften slightly, 3 to 4 minutes. Remove from heat and stir in the raw sugar and nutmeg. Evenly spread the pear mix into the tart shell. Sprinkle the white chocolate shavings all around the top of the tart. Bake for 45 minutes.

To prepare the sabayon:
While the tart is baking, combine the egg yolks, sugar, cardamom, and cava in a stainless steel bowl and place over a simmering pan of water on the stove. Be sure that the bowl fits the pan nicely, and that the ingredients in the bowl are over the water in the pan, not over the heat from the burner. Whisk constantly until the mixture becomes thick, pale, and creamy, about 10 to 15 minutes. Remove from heat and in a separate bowl whip the heavy cream, then fold it into the sabayon. Serve immediately over the freshly baked tart.

Cookies

½ cup powdered sugar

1 cup (2 sticks) butter, softened

½ teaspoon peppermint extract

1 ½ cups flour

½ cup cornstarch

Frosting

½ cup cream cheese, softened

¼ cup (½ stick) butter, softened

½ teaspoon peppermint extract

2 to 3 cups powdered sugar

¼ cup water

Makes 2 dozen

Peppermint Meltaways

COFFEE POT BAKERY CAFÉ, FOUR CORNERS
CHEF MARCI GEHRING

Perfect for a seasonal cookie that fits right into the winter holiday celebrations, this recipe is also amazingly adaptable. Experiment with flavor by substituting maple syrup, espresso, or orange concentrate for the peppermint extract in the cookie and frosting, or replace half of the flour with cocoa powder for a chocolate cookie.

To prepare the cookies:
Preheat the oven to 350 degrees.

In a large bowl, combine the powdered sugar, butter, and peppermint extract and beat until creamy. Add the flour and cornstarch and mix well. Shape into 1-inch balls, "thumbprint" each cookie in the middle, and place on a baking sheet. Bake for 12 to 15 minutes. Remove and allow to cool on wire racks.

To prepare the frosting:
Combine the cream cheese, butter, peppermint extract, and powdered sugar in a stand mixer until smooth and thick. Add the water 1 tablespoon at a time until you achieve the piping consistency. Use a pastry bag and ½-inch tip to pipe the frosting into the "thumbprint" on the cooled cookies. Or apply a dollop of frosting to each cookie with a tablespoon.

❧ *Chef's Tip: Sprinkle crushed candy canes (for peppermint) or toffee on top of the frosted cookies to add another layer of flavor.*

Red Velvet Cupcakes

JJ'S BAKERY, GREAT FALLS   ❧   CHEF JOHN WILLIAMS

Simply rich, elegantly delectable.

Preheat the oven to 350 degrees.

In a large mixing bowl, sift together the flour, cocoa, baking powder, baking soda, and salt. Set aside. In the bowl of a stand mixer, blend the butter and sugar, then add the eggs. Mix in the buttermilk, food coloring, and vinegar. Add the flour mixture and blend thoroughly, being careful not to over-mix. Spoon the batter into nine large cupcake papers in a muffin tin or a 9 x 13-inch greased pan and bake —30 to 35 minutes for cupcakes or 45 minutes for pan. Remove from the oven and cool on a wire rack. Top with Cream Cheese Frosting.

2½ cups flour

¼ cup cocoa

1 teaspoon baking powder

1 teaspoon baking soda

1 teaspoon salt

½ cup (1 stick) butter

1½ cups sugar

2 eggs

1 cup buttermilk

1 tablespoon red food coloring

1 teaspoon vinegar

Cream Cheese Frosting
(see recipe on page 132)

Makes 9 large cupcakes

LIFE ON THE FARM: HUTTERITES

At farmers' markets throughout Montana, the sight of Hutterite vans or buses loaded with freshly harvested produce is common. Hutterites rely on farming as their economic mainstay, producing hogs, beef, dairy, eggs, poultry, and grain. They also sell to local grocery stores and restaurants.

Much like their Amish brethren in the East, Hutterites speak German and live communally, sharing all property and proceeds from their efforts equally among members of their colony. There are fifty colonies in the state with about 100 residents in each community, all of whom contribute to life on the farm. They are a Protestant religious sect that shuns material possessions and uses technology only to better the community as a whole.

Pastry

1 cup whole-grain pastry flour

½ cup all-purpose flour

1 tablespoon sugar

¼ teaspoon kosher salt

2 cups (4 sticks) butter, chilled

2 tablespoons ice-cold water

Filling

1 pound Flathead cherries, pitted

½ cup sugar

3 tablespoons cornstarch

⅛ teaspoon salt

1 tablespoon lemon zest

½ teaspoon vanilla extract

1 tablespoon butter, chilled

Serves 8

"Flathead" is not a variety of cherry tree. Flathead refers to the region around Montana's famous Flathead Lake, where many varieties of cherries are grown, including Lapin, Rainier, Sweetheart, Van, Stella, Lambert, and Skeena.

Rustic Flathead Cherry Tart

SEABRING DAVIS, LIVINGSTON

There are few things as satisfying as picking your own Flathead cherries up north. When the cherries are in season, it feels like a true gift of summer. The rustic element of this dessert comes from the free-form aspect of the dough—no fancy tart pan required here.

To prepare the pastry:

In a medium bowl, whisk together the whole-wheat pastry flour, all-purpose flour, sugar, and kosher salt. Using two knives or a pastry cutter, cut the butter into the flour mixture until you get a pebbly, coarse texture. Using a fork, gradually mix in the water. Pat the dough into a 4-inch round and wrap in plastic wrap. Refrigerate for 30 minutes.

To prepare the filling:

In a large bowl, combine the cherries, sugar, cornstarch, salt, lemon zest, and vanilla extract and toss to evenly coat the cherries. Set aside.

To assemble the tart:

Preheat the oven to 400 degrees. Prepare a baking sheet by covering it with parchment paper. On a lightly floured surface, roll the dough evenly into a 10- to 12-inch round shape. Place the rolled dough onto the parchment paper. Arrange the cherries in a mound in the center of the dough, leaving a 2-inch border. Fold the border over the filling. The pastry will only partially cover the fruit and does not need to be even. Place dots of butter on top of the filling.

Bake the tart at 400 degrees for 15 minutes, then reduce the tempera-ture to 350 degrees and bake until the crust is golden brown, another 40 minutes. Serve warm.

Cake

3 eggs

1 cup vegetable oil

2 cups sugar

1¼ teaspoons vanilla extract

2 cups plus 1 tablespoon flour

1 teaspoon salt

1 teaspoon baking soda

3 cups chopped apples

1 cup chopped nuts (your choice)

Frosting

½ cup brown sugar

¼ cup cream

Serves 12

Shenandoah Apple Cake

PINE BUTTE GUEST RANCH, CHOTEAU ❧ MISS LOLA

Run by The Nature Conservancy, this landmark guest ranch takes pride in the extensive gardens on the property that provide for meals at the ranch. Whenever possible, the chef uses fresh-picked apples for this simple cake.

To prepare the cake:
Preheat the oven to 350 degrees.

In a large bowl, combine the eggs, vegetable oil, sugar, and vanilla extract and beat for 3 minutes. In a separate bowl, combine the 2 cups of flour, salt, and baking soda. Add the flour mixture to the wet ingredients and stir in the apples, nuts, and remaining 1 tablespoon of flour.

Pour the batter into a greased 9 x 13–inch pan. Bake for 1 hour, then cool for 30 minutes.

To prepare the frosting:
In a small saucepan, combine the brown sugar and cream and bring to a boil. Hold the boil for 3 minutes, stirring constantly. Pour the hot frosting over the top of the cooled cake. Serve warm.

Pudding

1½ cups chopped pitted dates

1¼ cups water

1 teaspoon baking soda

1½ cups sifted flour

1 teaspoon baking powder

½ teaspoon sea salt

¼ cup (½ stick) butter,
    room temperature

1 cup sugar

1 teaspoon vanilla extract

2 eggs

Sauce

1¼ cups light brown sugar,
    packed tightly

½ cup heavy cream

¼ cup (½ stick) butter

1 good glug of bourbon

½ teaspoon vanilla extract

1 cup heavy cream,
    to drizzle on cake

Serves 8 to 10

Sticky Toffee Pudding

MONTANA JACK'S BAR AND GRILL, DEAN
CHEF CHRIS LOCKHART

A cross between bread pudding and grandma's coffee cake, this dessert triggers comfort food bliss.

To prepare the pudding:
Preheat the oven to 350 degrees.

Butter and flour a 6-cup Bundt pan. In a medium-heavy saucepan with tall sides, bring the dates and 1¼ cups of water to a boil. Remove from heat and stir in the baking soda (the mixture will foam up). Set aside to cool.

In a small bowl, whisk together the flour, baking powder, and salt. In a separate, larger bowl, use an electric mixer to blend together the butter, sugar, and vanilla extract. Add one egg, half of the flour mixture, and half of the date mixture; beat to blend all ingredients. Repeat with the remaining egg, flour mixture, and date mixture. Pour the batter into the Bundt pan and bake until a toothpick inserted in the center comes out clean, 40 to 45 minutes.

To prepare the sauce:
Bring the brown sugar, cream, and butter to a boil in a small, heavy saucepan over medium heat, stirring constantly. Continue to boil, stirring constantly to prevent lumps, for 3 minutes. Remove from heat and stir in the bourbon and vanilla extract.

Cut the cake into wedges. Serve with the bourbon caramel sauce and a drizzle of heavy cream.

Crust

4 cups crushed cream-filled
   chocolate cookies (such as
   Oreos) or graham crackers

5 tablespoons butter, melted

Chocolate ganache

3 cups heavy cream

1 pound semi-sweet chocolate,
   chopped

Filling

5 to 6 cups softened
   Stuck in a Rut ice cream
   or your choice of flavor
   (even two different flavors)

1 cup crushed toffee

Serves 8

Stuck in a Rut Mud Pie

SEABRING DAVIS, LIVINGSTON

Mud pie is meant to be easy and playful, just the way it sounds. Any combination of ice cream works for this no-bake crowd-pleaser dessert. This version uses Wilcoxson's ice cream, which is headquartered in Livingston and proudly served in parts of Montana and Wyoming. In 2012 the business celebrated a century of making ice cream. Second-generation owner Harold Wilcoxson commemorated the milestone with the specialty ice cream Stuck in a Rut: "We've been Stuck in a Rut for 100 Years."

To prepare the crust:
Generously spray a 9-inch pie plate (preferably glass) with cooking spray. (A 10-inch springform pan with removable bottom also works well.) Combine 3 cups of crushed cookies with the melted butter and press into the bottom and sides of the pie plate to form a crust. Place in the freezer to firm up, approximately 30 minutes.

To prepare the chocolate ganache:
In a medium saucepan, heat the heavy cream to a simmer and add the chocolate. Remove from heat and let stand for 2 minutes. Stir until smooth and set aside.

To prepare the filling:
Spoon 3 cups of softened ice cream into a bowl. Mix by hand until it is the consistency of an ultra-thick milkshake. Remove the crust from the freezer and spread half of the ice cream into the pie plate, using a rubber spatula. Sprinkle this first layer with the remaining crushed cookies and ½ cup crushed toffee. Add the remainder of the ice cream, spreading it carefully. Slowly pour the ganache on top, spreading evenly. Sprinkle with the remaining toffee. Return to the freezer overnight.

To serve, remove the mud pie from the freezer to soften for 15 minutes before slicing.

Cook's Pantry

Rose Hip Jam, p. 138

3 egg yolks

1 tablespoon heavy cream

1 tablespoon fresh lemon juice

½ cup (1 stick) butter, melted and cooled to room temperature

Salt and pepper

Makes 1 cup

Basic Hollandaise Sauce

Prepare this classic hollandaise sauce with Parmesan Pain Perdu Benedict (see recipe in the Breakfast & Brunch chapter, page 9).

Prepare a double boiler on the stove; bring water to a simmer. If you don't have a double boiler, place a metal bowl over a pot of water; be sure the water does not touch the bottom of the bowl. Do not boil or eggs will become too hot and begin to scramble.

In a metal bowl, whisk the egg yolks and cream together until well combined. Place over the simmering pot or in the double boiler and whisk continuously, but gently, until the liquid thickens, 2 to 4 minutes. Remove from heat.

Pour the fresh lemon juice into the cooled melted butter. Slowly add this mixture to the egg mixture while whisking constantly at an even pace. The sauce will thicken to a creamy texture. Stir in the salt and pepper to taste. Cover and keep warm until ready to serve.

1 cup flour

2 eggs, beaten

Makes about 2 dozen ravioli

Basic Pasta Dough

CHICO HOT SPRINGS RESORT, PRAY   CHEF MORGAN MILTON

These are the basic ingredients for making pasta by hand. Although most egg pasta recipes use this formula, the secrets to success are not in the ingredients but in the techniques. This method uses a hand-cranked pasta machine. Instructions for shaping ravioli are also given here. Use this pasta dough for the ravioli in Barbecue Bison Short Rib Ravioli (see recipe in the Appetizers & Snacks chapter, page 17).

Place the flour into a large bowl, form it into a well, and put the beaten eggs in the center, mixing in the flour with a wooden spoon. Then knead vigorously for 8 to 10 minutes, starting in the bowl and moving to a countertop. (Do not skimp on kneading the dough; most problems with pasta dough stem from insufficient kneading.)

When the dough is smooth and silky, wrap it in plastic wrap and let rest for at least 30 minutes or up to 2 hours. This step is important—the dough must rest so it can be stretched. Unwrap, dust your hands with flour (don't add more flour to the dough, although it will seem moist), and knead for 1 minute more.

To prepare ravioli:
Cut the pasta into four pieces and flatten each. Cover three loosely with plastic wrap on a board (don't refrigerate). Open the roller on the pasta machine to the widest plain setting and lightly dust the fourth piece of pasta with flour. Run it through the roller two to three times until flattened and smooth. Then reduce the width and run the pasta through again. Repeat until the dough is very thin, usually at setting 3 or less. Lay the thin pasta sheet onto your work area.

Using a tablespoon, mound the ravioli filling down the middle of the pasta sheet, leaving an inch of space between each mound. Run a second piece of pasta through the roller until thin, then place it over the first pasta sheet, covering the filling. Place a 2½-inch round cookie cutter over the filling mounds and press hard enough to cut through the pasta. Crimp the edges around each circle to seal. Repeat this process with the remaining two pieces of pasta. Cook immediately, refrigerate for same-day use, or freeze.

¼ cup fresh thyme

¼ cup fresh parsley

¼ cup fresh rosemary

¼ cup fresh sage

¼ cup fresh garlic

1 pound kosher salt

Makes 2 cups

½ cup white wine vinegar

2 tablespoons Dijon-style mustard

1 tablespoon honey

Salt

¾ teaspoon freshly ground
   black pepper

1 cup canola oil

Makes nearly 2 cups

Bistro Seasoning Salt

2ND STREET BISTRO, LIVINGSTON
CHEF/PROPRIETOR BRIAN MENGES

This is a wonderful all-purpose seasoning, but be careful using it with seafood, as it can overpower a delicate fish. Try it in the Lamb Ragout with Pappardelle (see recipe in the Main Courses chapter, page 80).

Puree all the ingredients in a blender or food processer, and then mix well. Store in an airtight container in the refrigerator.

Black Pepper Vinaigrette

PARADISE VALLEY GRILL, LIVINGSTON   ⚘   CHEF JOSH PASTRAMA

This versatile dressing is a great staple to have on hand in the refrigerator. Chef Pastrama serves it with Roasted Beet Salad with Black Pepper Vinaigrette (see recipe in the Salads & Sides chapter, page 49), but it is compatible with any salad.

Place the vinegar, mustard, honey, salt, and pepper in a blender and blend until smooth. Remove the lid and slowly add the canola oil, drizzling it into the blender to create a smooth emulsification. Pour into a lidded container and refrigerate.

1 ¼ cups flour

1 tablespoon sugar

¼ teaspoon salt

½ cup (1 stick) cold butter

3 tablespoons cold water

1 teaspoon fresh lemon juice

Makes 1 (10-inch) pie crust

Butter Crust Pie Dough

This is the perfect pie crust to accompany Coconut Cream Pie (see recipe in the Desserts & Sweet Treats chapter, page 102).

In a large bowl, combine the flour, sugar, and salt. Cut the butter into ¼-inch cubes and, using a pastry cutter or two knives, cut the butter into the flour mixture until the texture is similar to coarse cornmeal, with pieces the size of peas. Add the water and lemon juice and mix with your hands until the dough just holds together. Do not overwork.

Divide dough in two and shape into ½-inch-thick disks. Let rest for at least 30 minutes before rolling.

To prebake the crust:
Preheat the oven to 350 degrees. Line a 9- or 10-inch pie pan with dough. Brush the bottom and edges with milk to keep the crust from becoming too dark, then line the rim with aluminum foil or a pie ring. Mound uncooked dry beans on the crust over the bottom of the pan as a pie weight, to prevent bubbles from forming during cooking. Bake until golden brown, 25 to 30 minutes. Remove from the oven and allow to cool.

The dough can be frozen uncooked for 2 months.

¼ cup red wine

¼ cup extra virgin olive oil

2 garlic cloves

½ teaspoon red pepper flakes

2 teaspoons fresh oregano,
    or 1 teaspoon dry oregano

1 teaspoon ground cumin

1 cup chopped fresh flat-leaf parsley

1 cup chopped fresh cilantro

Salt and pepper

Makes 2 cups

Chimmichurri Sauce

MOUNTAIN SKY GUEST RANCH, EMIGRANT
CHEF BRIAN BIELEN

Originally from Argentina, chimmichurri is a versatile sauce used primarily with grilled red meat, but it also works well with fish and chicken. It's used here to accompany Grilled Rack of Lamb with Chimmichurri Sauce (see recipe in Main Courses chapter, page 78).

Combine all the ingredients in a blender and puree until smooth. The sauce is best served fresh, but will keep for 2 days at room temperature or up to a week in the refrigerator.

❧ ***Chef's Tip:*** *The sauce is best served at room temperature to enjoy the fullest flavor of the fresh herbs and garlic.*

Cooking spray

1 egg

1 tablespoon water

1 package puff pastry dough

Makes 1 (10-inch) pie crust

Coconut Cream Pie Crust

POMPEY'S GRILL, SACAJAWEA HOTEL, THREE FORKS
CHEF MATTHEW ISRAEL

Use this puff pastry crust for the chef's presentation of the Coconut Cream Pie on page 102.

Preheat the oven to 375 degrees.

Generously coat a pie pan with cooking spray. In a separate dish, mix the egg and water.

Unfold one pastry square on a lightly floured surface. Roll the pastry firmly to remove creases, keeping the square shape. Press the pastry into the pie pan, allowing the corners to drape over the edges. Prick the center of the pastry with a fork and brush with the egg wash. Bake until golden brown, 20 to 25 minutes.

Remove from the oven. With the back of a spoon, press an indent down the center of the hot pastry. Cool in the pan on a wire rack for 15 to 20 minutes.

1 cup dried cranberries

1 cup cranberry juice

1 cup sugar

1 cup cabernet wine

4 cups beef broth

Makes 8 cups

Cranberry Reduction Sauce

PARADISE VALLEY GRILL, LIVINGSTON ❧ CHEF JOSH PASTRAMA

Use this tangy sauce for Maple-Brined Pork Chops with Cranberry Reduction (see recipe in the Main Courses chapter, page 84).

In a medium-size saucepan, bring all the ingredients to a boil and then lower the heat to a simmer. Reduce the sauce until it is what the French call nape. Nape means "to coat the back of a spoon." When you dip a spoon into the sauce and remove it, you should be able to draw a line with your finger in the sauce clinging to the spoon, leaving the remaining sauce on either side of the line. Once your sauce is at this consistency, set it aside and reheat when ready to plate.

½ cup (1 stick) butter, softened

1 cup (8 ounces) cream cheese, softened

2 teaspoons vanilla extract (clear vanilla will keep frosting very white)

4 cups powdered sugar

Makes 3 cups

Cream Cheese Frosting

HANGIN' ART GALLERY, ARLEE   &   CHEF DONNA MOLLICA

*Use this decadent frosting for Carrot Cake and Red Velvet Cupcakes
(see recipes in the Desserts & Sweet Treats chapter, page 99 and page 119).*

In a blender or stand mixer, combine the butter, cream cheese, and vanilla extract. Add the powdered sugar and blend until soft and creamy, 3 to 5 minutes. Use a bit more or less powdered sugar to get the consistency you want for the frosting.

1 cup heavy whipping cream, room temperature

1 tablespoon buttermilk, or ½ cup sour cream, room temperature

Makes 1½ cups

Crème Fraîche

CAFÉ DECAMP, BILLINGS   &   CHEF/PROPRIETOR JASON DECAMP

In an interesting twist, crème fraîche is used here in Huckleweizen Beer Ice Cream (see recipe in the Desserts & Sweet Treats chapter, page 110).

Pour the heavy whipping cream and buttermilk (or sour cream) into a jar with a threaded lid. Secure the lid tightly and shake for 15 seconds. Set aside at room temperature for 24 hours or until very thick. Stir once or twice during that time.

Stir thickened crème fraîche well. Refrigerate at least 6 hours before serving. Cover tightly and store in the refrigerator for up to 2 weeks.

& **Chef's Tip:** *The cream will thicken faster if the room is warm.*

Basic béchamel

3 tablespoons butter

2 to 3 tablespoons flour

2 cups whole milk

1 teaspoon kosher salt

Pepper

Honey-butter sauce

⅓ cup Parmesan cheese, shredded

½ teaspoon white pepper

1 teaspoon kosher salt

¼ cup plus 1 teaspoon
fresh lemon juice

½ cup (1 stick) butter

2 tablespoons honey

1 teaspoon red pepper flakes

1 tablespoon parsley flakes

1 teaspoon freshly ground
black pepper

Makes 2 cups

Honey-Butter Béchamel Sauce

CONTINENTAL DIVIDE RESTAURANT & BISTRO, ENNIS
CHEF/PROPRIETOR ERIC TRAPP

*Use for the Macadamia-Crusted Fresh Wild Walleye (see recipe in the
Main Courses chapter, page 81).*

To prepare the basic béchamel:
In a medium saucepan, melt the butter over medium heat. Sprinkle
the flour into the butter, whisking constantly until smooth. Cook
on medium until slightly golden, 4 to 6 minutes. Heat the milk in
a separate saucepan and bring to a simmer. Add the hot milk to
the butter 1 cup at a time, whisking constantly until smooth.

Bring the mixture to a boil, then simmer for 10 minutes on low.
Salt and pepper to taste.

To prepare the honey-butter sauce:
Whisk the Parmesan cheese into the basic béchamel; season with
white pepper, kosher salt, and 1 teaspoon of fresh lemon juice.
Continue to whisk, adding the butter 1 tablespoon at a time,
until each is melted. Add the honey, ¼ cup of fresh lemon juice,
red pepper flakes, parsley flakes, and freshly ground black pepper.
Whisk thoroughly, then keep the sauce in a warm spot until it is
served. It should look like a beurre blanc.

❧ *Chef's Tip: This is not a classic preparation—the sauce is a lighter consistency
than a classic sauce and not as rich or acidulated as a butter sauce. Whisk
it occasionally, and once again immediately before serving. If it breaks, try
whisking in a teaspoon of water. If it does break despite your efforts, serve
it anyway. It will not keep overnight.*

4 cups huckleberry juice

1 cup milk

2 cups heavy cream

6 egg yolks

¾ cup sugar

Pinch salt

Serves 10 to 12

Huckleberry Crème Anglaise

TWO SISTERS CAFÉ, BABB   ❧   CHEF SUSAN HIGGINS

Use as an optional topping for Huckleberry-Lemon Bread Pudding (see recipe in the Desserts & Sweet Treats chapter, page 106). This recipe also makes a perfect ice cream custard. After cooling overnight, simply freeze the mixture according to your electric machine directions.

Drain 4 cups of juice from frozen berries or from fresh berries processed in a blender with ¼ cup water. In a large saucepan over low heat, reduce the huckleberry juice by 75 percent (you should end up with 1 cup of syrup).

Heat the milk and cream until simmering. In a separate bowl, whisk the egg yolks, sugar, and salt until the mixture is a light buttery yellow and slightly thickened. Temper the egg yolk mixture with hot cream by slowly adding small amounts of cream (about half the cream mixture total) while whisking constantly. Placing a damp dish towel under the bowl holding the egg yolks will keep it stable, and a ladle is the perfect tool to add the cream to the yolks.

After the eggs have warmed, whisk in the rest of the cream. Transfer the custard mixture to a large saucepan and carefully heat over medium heat, stirring gently and constantly, until it forms a thick coating on the back of a wooden spoon. Do not let this mixture come to a boil or overheat it, as the eggs will scramble and you will have a lumpy sauce. Strain the sauce through a fine sieve or cheesecloth and cool completely.

❧ *Chef's Tip: If you overcook your sauce and scramble the eggs, all is not lost. Strain the sauce through cheesecloth (a sieve will not get all the scrambled egg) and cool. Be patient—this will take awhile. Do not press the mixture while straining; stir gently.*

Lemon Chiffon Cake

TWO SISTERS CAFÉ, BABB ❧ CHEF SUSAN HIGGINS

Prepare this cake in advance to incorporate into Huckleberry-Lemon Bread Pudding (see recipe in the Desserts & Sweet Treats chapter, page 106).

2 cups flour

1 ½ cups sugar

3 teaspoons baking powder

1 teaspoon salt

½ cup cold water

¼ cup fresh lemon juice

½ cup vegetable oil

2 teaspoons vanilla extract

2 teaspoons grated lemon peel

8 eggs, separated

Makes 2 (8 x 8-inch) cakes

Preheat the oven to 325 degrees.

Sift the flour, sugar, baking powder, and salt in the bowl of a stand mixer.

Add the water, lemon juice, oil, vanilla extract, lemon peel, and egg yolks. Blend until smooth and remove to another bowl. In a very clean, dry mixing bowl, beat the egg whites until stiff peaks form. Do not overbeat! If you see liquid on the bottom of the mixing bowl, throw it out and start over.

Transfer the egg whites into a large mixing bowl. Slowly fold in the egg yolk batter with a rubber spatula until just blended. Divide the batter into two 8 x 8-inch cake pans lined with parchment and sprayed with nonstick cooking spray.

Bake for 30 to 35 minutes. The cakes are done when the color is an even golden brown, the sides have pulled away from the pan, and the top springs back when gently pressed. Cool upside down on a wire rack and remove from cake pans when *completely* cooled.

1 yellow onion, finely diced

2 tablespoons butter

¼ cup minced garlic

½ teaspoon crushed
    red pepper flakes

1½ teaspoons black pepper

1 tablespoon blackening
    (Cajun) spice

1 (12-ounce) bottle
    Moose Drool beer

¾ cup apple cider vinegar

¼ cup molasses

1 tablespoon Worcestershire sauce

2 dashes Tabasco sauce

4 cups ketchup

Makes 4 cups

Buffalo meat is lower in fat,
calories, and cholesterol and higher
in protein than most other meats.
There are roughly 130 private
buffalo ranches in Montana,
several of which sell meat to
restaurants and directly to buyers.

Moose Drool Barbecue Sauce

CHICO HOT SPRINGS RESORT, PRAY CHEF MORGAN MILTON

*Whip up a batch of this sauce to accompany the Barbecue Bison Short
Rib Ravioli (see recipe in the Main Courses chapter, page 17).*

In a large heavy-walled stockpot, brown the onions in butter over
low heat for about 5 minutes. Add the garlic and cook until very
brown, another 3 to 5 minutes. Add the red pepper flakes, black
pepper, and blackening spice and stir well. Pour in the beer and
vinegar and continue to cook until reduced by one-third. Add the
molasses, Worcestershire sauce, Tabasco sauce, and ketchup, bring
to a boil, and reduce heat to a simmer for 10 minutes.

2 ½ cups all-purpose unbleached
flour (local and organic,
if possible)

2 ½ cups whole-wheat pastry flour
(local and organic, if possible)

2 tablespoons salt

2 tablespoons sugar

¾ cup shortening

¾ cup bacon fat (if available)
or salted butter

1 ½ cups ice water

Makes 12 pasties

Pasty Dough

BENNY'S BISTRO, HELENA
CHEF/PROPRIETOR MARGARET CORCORAN

*This versatile dough can be used with any combination of savory fillings.
Use it to make Cornish Pasties (see recipe in the Appetizers & Snacks
chapter, page 21).*

In a large mixing bowl, blend the two flours with the salt and
sugar. In another bowl, blend the shortening and bacon fat (or salted
butter). Add the fat to the flour and blend using your fingers, forks,
a pastry cutter, or whatever method your grandmother used, until
the dough is ragged in appearance. Gradually add the cold water
and gently mix by hand, until the mixture just comes together.
This is the hard part—not too dry and not too wet. Wrap the dough
in plastic and refrigerate until it's relaxed and chilled, about 1 hour
or up to 2 days.

2 cups fresh basil

4 garlic cloves

¼ cup pine nuts

½ cup extra virgin olive oil

½ cup Parmesan cheese

2 cups mayonnaise

Salt and pepper

Makes 2½ cups

Pesto-Mayo Dressing

GLACIER PARK LODGE, EAST GLACIER PARK
EXECUTIVE CHEF MICHAEL GORSKI

This pesto is paired with the Red Potato and Walnut Salad (see recipe in the Salads & Sides chapter, page 47), but it is also perfect for chicken salad, pasta salad, or even as a creative spread on gourmet sandwiches.

Combine the basil, garlic, and pine nuts in a food processor; pulse 3 to 4 times. Slowly add the oil while pulsing to combine. Add the cheese and pulse to blend, creating a pesto base. Mix with the mayonnaise and season to taste with salt and pepper. Cover and refrigerate for later use.

1 ½ cups sugar

¼ cup water

½ tablespoon pectin

2 cups rose hips

¼ cup rosé or muscat wine

Makes 1 cup

Rose Hip Jam

J BAR L RANCH, LIMA   &   CHEF ANDREW IRVIN-ERICKSON

Prepare in advance to use with Skirt Steak with Rose Hip Jam and Burnt Grapes (see recipe in the Main Courses chapter, page 92).

Simmer the sugar, water, and pectin until they form a thick syrup. Add the rose hips and turn the heat as low as possible. Allow to steep 10 minutes and add the wine. Cool and refrigerate overnight.

(see photograph on page 125)

¾ cup (6 ounces) cream cheese

1 cup (2 sticks) butter

2½ cups flour

¼ cup milk, to brush on top crust

Makes 2 (9-inch) pie crusts

Savory Pie Crust

CHICO HOT SPRINGS RESORT, PRAY   ❧   CHEF MORGAN MILTON

The combination of cream cheese and butter make this a foolproof pie crust that's a perfect fit for savory fillings, such as Savory Tomato Pie (see recipe in the Salads & Sides chapter, page 51). It's also versatile enough to use for berry fillings that need a firmer crust to stand up to all that juice.

In a stand mixer with a paddle attachment, blend the cream cheese and butter until well combined. Add the flour, mix until a dough ball forms, and remove from the bowl. Divide into two balls, flatten, and wrap in plastic wrap. Refrigerate for 45 minutes.

On a lightly floured surface, use a rolling pin to roll out the disks of dough into 11-inch rounds.

To prebake a crust, preheat the oven to 350 degrees. Line a 9-inch pie pan with dough. Brush the bottom and edges with milk to keep the crust from becoming too dark, then line the rim with aluminum foil or a pie ring. Mound uncooked dry beans on the crust in the bottom of the pan as a pie weight, to prevent bubbles from forming during cooking. Bake until golden brown, 25 to 30 minutes. Remove from the oven and allow to cool.

The dough can be frozen uncooked for 2 months.

Chicken stock

1 sweet onion, diced medium

1 carrot, diced medium

2 celery stalks, diced medium

6 garlic cloves, cleaned and halved

1 cup dry white wine

2 bay leaves

1 whole chicken

1 lemon, halved

5 quarts water

Mushroom stock

2 pints crimini mushrooms, chopped

4 cups water

2 bay leaves

Salt and pepper

Makes 11 cups

Tag Sauce

LATITUDE 48°, WHITEFISH ❧ CHEF JAMES TRAVIS MANNING

Use this sauce for Tagliatelle with Wild Mushrooms (see recipe in the Main Courses chapter, page 95).

To prepare the chicken stock:
Sear the vegetables and garlic in a large stockpot until lightly cara-melized and then deglaze with white wine. Add the bay leaves and cook for 5 more minutes, then add the chicken, lemon, and 5 quarts of water. Simmer this mixture for 30 minutes, then remove the chicken and cool. Once cool enough to handle, pull the edible meat off the breast, legs, and thighs and reserve for the final dish. Return the carcass to the cooking liquid and simmer for another 2 to 4 hours, until the liquid tastes strongly of chicken. Once flavorful, strain though a fine sieve and cool as quickly as possible.

To prepare the mushroom stock:
In a large stockpot, combine the mushrooms and water and bring to a simmer. Continue to simmer until reduced by a quarter (about 2 hours), then strain through a fine sieve. Cool as quickly as possible.

To prepare the Tag sauce:
Combine both stocks and the bay leaves and simmer until reduced by half. Season to taste, strain though a fine sieve, and cool as quickly as possible.

❧ *Chef's Tip: If this recipe makes more stock than required, freeze the remainder in small amounts and thaw as needed for a household chicken stock/broth. It's a great substitute for store-bought bouillon cubes.*

2 cups flour

½ teaspoon salt

¾ cup (1½ sticks) butter,
   chilled and cut into
   ¼-inch cubes

¼ cup Crisco shortening,
   in four pieces

6 to 8 tablespoons ice water

Makes 1 (9-inch) tart crust

Tart Crust

THE PEARL CAFÉ, MISSOULA ❧ CHEF PEARL CASH

Use this crust as the base for Lemon Curd Tart with Huckleberry Sauce (see recipe in the Desserts & Sweet Treats chapter, page 113).

Sift the flour and salt together, then cut in the butter and Crisco with a pastry blender or two knives until chunky—don't over-blend. Stir in the water until the dough just holds together. Pat gently into a round, wrap in plastic, and refrigerate for 1 hour.

To prebake, preheat the oven to 350 degrees. On a lightly floured surface, roll out the dough and place in a 9-inch tart pan. Place a circle of parchment paper in the tart shell and top with dry beans or pie weights, to prevent bubbles from forming during cooking. Bake until lightly browned, about 15 minutes. Remove the beans and cool.

sources

AERO Montana
432 North Last Chance Gulch
Helena, MT 59601
(406) 443-7272
aeromt.org

Agnew Ranch Grass-fed Lamb
781 Lower Sweet Grass Road
Big Timber, MT 59011
(406) 932-6503
agnewranch.com

Amaltheia Organic Dairy
3380 Penwell Bridge Road
Belgrade, MT 59714
(406) 388-5950
amaltheiadairy.com

B Bar Ranch
818 Tom Miner Creek Road
Emigrant, MT 59027
(406) 848-7729
bbar.com

Blue Moon Orchard
Maureen McGraw and
Daniel Reisenfeld
1397 Wheelbarrow Creek Road
Stevensville, MT 59870
(406) 777-3326

Bowman Orchards
19944 Montana Highway 35
Bigfork, MT 59911
(406) 982-3246
bowmancherries.com

Bozeman Community Food Co-op
908 West Main
Bozeman, MT 59715
(406) 587-4039
bozo.coop.com

Broken Willow Bison Ranch
702 US Highway 89 North
White Sulphur Springs, MT 59645
(406) 547-2240
brokenwillowbisonranch.com

Dixon Melons
Harley and Joey Hettick
P.O. Box 13
Dixon, MT 59831-0013
(406) 246-3526
dixonmelons.com

Drange Apiaries
2751 Alpine View Drive
Laurel, MT 59044
(406) 855-4868
(406) 628-8839

Farm-to-Table Store
313 South Merrill
Glendive, MT 59330
(406) 377-4284
farmtotablecoop.com

Fat Robin Orchard & Farm
34126 South Finley Point Road
Polson, MT 59860
(406) 887-2869
fatrobinorchard.com

Field Day Farms
P.O. Box 6357
Bozeman, MT 59771
(406) 522-9501
fielddayfarms.com

Gallatin Valley Botanical
P.O. Box 11745
Bozeman, MT 59719
(406) 599-2361
gallatinvalleybotanical.com

Garden City Fungi
P.O. Box 1591
Missoula, MT 59806
(406) 626-5757
gardencityfungi.com

Good Earth Market
3024 2nd Avenue North
Billings, MT 59101
(406) 259-2622
goodearthmarket.coop

Good Food Store
1600 South 3rd Street West
Missoula, MT 59801
(406) 541-3663
goodfoodstore.com

Grow Montana
432 North Last Chance Gulch
Helena, MT 59601
(406) 443-7272
growmontana.ncat.org

Indreland Ranch Natural Angus Beef
170 Glasson Road
Big Timber, MT 59011
(406) 932-4232
indrelandranchangusbeef.com

Kalispell Kreamery
480 Lost Creek Drive
Kalispell, MT 59901
(406) 756-6455
kalispellkreamery.com

Lazy SR Ranch
729 Shields River Road
Wilsall, MT 59086
(406) 578-2330
lazysrranch.com

Lifeline Farm
2533 Pleasant View Drive
Victor, MT 59875
(406) 642-9717
lifelinefarm.com

Made in Montana
madeinmontanausa.com

Mission Mountain Winery
82420 US Highway 93
P.O. Box 100
Dayton, MT 59914
(406) 849-5524
missionmountainwinery.com

Montana Fish Company
119 East Main Street
Bozeman, MT 59715
(406) 556-0200
montanafishcompany.com

Montana Organic Producers
1350 Custer Gulch Road
Lavin, MT 59046
(406) 667-2332
mopcoop.org

Omega Beef, Inc.
29 Bones Lane
Birney, MT 59012
(406) 984-6229
jcazc@rengeweb.net

Orchard at Flathead Lake
23126 Yellow Bay Lane
Bigfork, MT 59911
(406) 982-3058
montanaorchard.com

Pike Place Fish Market
Seattle, Washington
(800) 542-7732
pikeplacefish.com

Purple Frog Gardens
170 Blanchard Lake Drive
Whitefish, MT 59937
(406) 862-0621
purplefroggardens.com

Real Food Market and Deli
1096 Helena Avenue
Helena, MT 59601
(406) 443-5150
realfoodstore.com

Sabo Ranch Grass-fed Beef
P.O. Box 65
Harrison, MT 59735
(406) 685-3248
saboranch.com

Ten Spoon Vineyard
4175 Rattlesnake Drive
Missoula, MT 59802
(877) 549-8703
tenspoon.com

Timeless Seeds, Inc.
P.O. Box 881
Conrad, MT 59425
(406) 278-5722
timelessfood.com

Trout Culture, Inc.
P.O. Box 321
Virginia City, MT 59755
(406) 763-6328
troutculture.com

Western Montana
Growers Cooperative
P.O. Box 292
Arlee, MT 59821
(406) 726-4769
wmgcoop.com

Western Sustainability Exchange
Farm to Restaurant Program
P.O. Box 1448
Livingston, MT 59047
(406) 222-0730
westernsustainabilityexchange.com

Western Trails Food
313 West Valentine
Glendive, MT 59330
(406) 377-4284
westerntrailsfood.com

Wheat Montana
10778 Highway 287
Three Forks, MT 59752
(406) 285-3614
wheatmontana.com

Wilcoxson's Ice Cream Company
314 South Main Street
Livingston, MT 59047-3417
(406) 222-2370
wilcoxsonsicecream.com

Wild Echo Bison Ranch
P.O. Box 890
Townsend, MT 59644
(406) 202-2377
wildechobison.com

Wolf Ridge Lamb and Wool
850 East River Road
Pray, Montana 59065
(406) 333-4031
wolfridgeicelandics.com

Yellowstone Caviar
Glendive Chamber of
Commerce & Agriculture
808 North Merrill
Glendive, MT 59330
(406) 377-5601
glendivechamber.com

Yellowstone Grass-fed Beef
P.O. Box 253
Bozeman, MT 59771
(406) 599-9024
yellowstonegrassfedbeef.com

Yellowstone Valley Brewing Company
2123 1st Ave North, #B
Billings, MT 59101
(406) 245-0918
yellowstonevalleybrew.com

contributors

2nd Street Bistro
123 North 2nd Street
Livingston, MT 59047
(406) 222-9463
secondstreetbistro.com

Belton Chalet
12575 US Highway 2 East
P.O. Box 206
West Glacier, MT 59936
(406) 888-5000
beltonchalet.com

Benny's Bistro
108 East Sixth Avenue
Helena, MT 59601
(406) 443-0105
bennysbistro.com

Big Sky Resort
Peaks Restaurant
Carabiner Lounge
1 Lone Mountain Trail
Big Sky, MT 59716
(800) 548-4486
bigskyresort.com

Buck's T-4 Lodge
46625 Gallatin Road
(US Highway 191)
P.O. Box 160279
Big Sky, MT 59716
(406) 995-4111
buckst4.com

Café DeCamp
1404 6th Avenue North
Billings, MT 59101
(406) 256-7285
cafedecamp.com

Café Kandahar
3824 Big Mountain Road
Whitefish, MT 59937
(406) 862-6247
cafekandahar.com

Café Regis
501 South Word
Red Lodge, MT 59068
(406) 446-1941
caferegis.com

La Chatelaine Chocolat Co.
Main Store: 1516 West Main Street
La Petite shop: Baxter Hotel Lobby
105 West Main Street
Bozeman, MT 59715
(406) 522-5440
chatelainechocolate.com

Chico Hot Springs Resort
163 Chico Road
Pray, MT 59065
(406) 333-4933
chicohotsprings.com

Coffee Pot Bakery Café
80795 Gallatin Road (US Highway 191)
Bozeman, MT 59718
(406) 522-7707
no website

**Continental Divide
Restaurant & Bistro**
47 East Geyser Street
Ennis, MT 59729
(406) 682-7600
no website

Crazy Mountain Inn
110 Main Street
Martinsdale, MT 59053
(406) 572-3307
CrazyMountainInn.com

Discovery Ski Area
180 Discovery Basin Road
Anaconda, MT 59711
(406) 563-2184
skidiscovery.com

Farm-to-Table Store
313 South Merrill
Glendive, MT 59330
(406) 377-4284
farmtotablecoop.com

Firehole Ranch
P.O. Box 686
West Yellowstone, MT 59758
(406) 646-7294
fireholeranch.com

Gibson Mansion Bed & Breakfast
823 39th Street
Missoula, MT 59803
(406) 251-1345
gibsonmansion.com

Gil's Goods
207 West Park Street
Livingston, MT 59047
(406) 222-4711
gilsgoods.com

Glacier Park Lodge
1 Midvale Creek Road
East Glacier Park, MT 59434
(406) 892-2525
glacierparkinc.com

Good Medicine Lodge
537 Wisconsin Avenue
Whitefish MT 59937
(406) 862-5488
(800) 860-5488
goodmedicinelodge.com

The Grand Hotel
139 McLeod Street
Big Timber, MT 59011
(406) 932-4459
thegrand-hotel.com

Hangin' Art Gallery
92555 Highway 93
Arlee, MT 59821
(406) 726-5005
hanginartgallery.com

Harper & Madison Bakery and Café
3115 10th Avenue North
Billings, MT 59101
(406) 281-8550
harperandmadison.com

Holland Lake Lodge
1947 Holland Lake Lodge Road
Condon, MT 59826
(406) 754-2282
hollandlakelodge.com

Izaak Walton Inn
290 Izaak Walton Inn Road
Essex, MT 59916
(406) 888-5700
izaakwaltoninn.com

J Bar L Ranch
98 Balkovetz Lane
Twin Bridges, MT 59754
(406) 276-3583
jbarl.com

JJ's Bakery
112 Central Avenue
Great Falls, MT 59401
(406) 727-5910
jjsbakerymt.com

John Bozeman's Bistro
125 West Main Street
Bozeman, MT 59715
(406) 587-4100
breakingpointe.wix.com/john-
bozemans-bistro

Kafé Utza
19 South 9th Street
Miles City, MT 59301
(406) 234-9821
kafeutza.com

Latitude 48°
147 Central Avenue
Whitefish, MT 59937
(406) 863-2323
latitude48bistro.com

Laughing Horse Lodge
P.O. Box 5082
71284 Highway 83
Swan Lake, MT 59911
(406) 886-2080
laughinghorselodge.com

Lone Mountain Ranch
750 Lone Mountain Ranch Road
Big Sky, MT 59716
(800) 514-4644
lonemountainranch.com

LouLa's Cafe
300 2nd Street East
Whitefish, MT 59937-2414
(406) 862-5614
loulascafe.com

Many Glacier Hotel
Glacier National Park, MT
(406) 732-4411
glacierparkinc.com

The Mint Bar and Cafe
27 East Main Street
Belgrade, MT 59714
(406) 388-1100
themintmt.com

Montana Aleworks
611 East Main Street
Bozeman, MT 59715
(406) 587-7700
montanaaleworks.com

Montana Jack's Bar & Grill
1383 Nye Road
Dean, MT 59028
mtjacks.com
(406) 328-4110

Mountain Sky Guest Ranch
P.O. Box 1219
Emigrant, MT 59027
(406) 333-4911
(800) 548-3392
mtnsky.com

Norris Hot Springs
Rural Route 84
Norris, MT 59745
(406) 685-3303
norrishotsprings.com

The Old Hotel
101 East 5th Avenue
Twin Bridges, MT 59754
(406) 684-5959
theoldhotel.com

Onyx Bar & Grill
The Calvert Hotel
216 7th Avenue South
Lewistown, MT 59457
(406) 535-5415
thecalverthotel.com

Paradise Valley Grill
5237 US Highway 89 South
Livingston, MT 59047
(406) 222-4815
paradisevalleygrill.com

Park Avenue Bakery
44 South Park Avenue
Helena, MT 59601
(406) 449-8424
parkavenuebakery.net

The Pearl Café
231 East Front Street
Missoula, MT 59802
(406) 541-0231
pearlcafe.us

Pine Butte Guest Ranch
351 South Fork Road
Choteau, MT 59422
(406) 466-2158
nature.org/pinebutte

The Pollard Hotel
2 North Broadway
Red Lodge, MT 59068
(406) 446-0001
thepollard.com

Rainbow Ranch Lodge
42950 Gallatin Road
Big Sky, MT 59730
(406) 995-4132
(800) 937-4132
rainbowranchbigsky.com

The Resort at Paws Up®
40060 Paws Up Road
Greenough, MT 59823
(406) 244-5320
(800) 473-0601
pawsup.com

Rising Sun Bistro
25 2nd Avenue West
Kalispell, MT 59901
(406) 755-7510
risingsunbistro.com

Rising Sun Motor Inn
Going-to-the-Sun Road
East Glacier Park, MT
P.O. Box 2025
Columbia Falls, MT 59912
(406) 732-5523
glacierparkinc.com

Sacajawea Hotel/ Pompey's Grill
5 North Main Street
Three Forks, MT 59752
(406) 285-6515
(888) 722-2529
sacajaweahotel.com

Timeless Seeds, Inc.
P.O. Box 881
Conrad, MT 59425
(406) 278-5722
timelessfood.com

Two Sisters Café
US Highway 89
P.O. Box 230
Babb, MT 59411
(406) 396-0537 (cell)
(406) 732-5535 (seasonal)
twosistersofmontana.com

Walker's American Grill and Tapas Bar
2700 1st Avenue North
Billings, MT 59101
(406) 245-9291
walkersgrill.com

Wheat Montana Deli
10778 Highway 287
Three Forks, MT 59752
(406) 285-3614
wheatmontana.com

Wild West Pizzeria
14 Madison Avenue
West Yellowstone, MT 59758
(406) 646-4400
wildwestpizza.com

The Windbag Saloon & Grill
19 North Last Chance Gulch
Helena, MT 59601
(406) 443-9669
no website

Yesterday's Calf-A
2 Main Street
Dell, MT 59724
(406) 276-3308
no website

index